THE 5,000 YEAR OLD MYSTERY

In 1840, there was a violent earthquake in Eastern Turkey. An expedition checking for damage discovered a gigantic wooden ship high atop Mt. Ararat.

In 1876, British statesman Sir James Bryce climbed Mt. Ararat alone and returned with a five-foot piece of hand-hewn timber.

In 1887, Prince John Joseph Nouri ascended Mt. Ararat and found a vessel with stalls and cages on board.

In 1955, French engineer Fernand Navarra brought back the first photographs of the mysterious ship.

In 1972, an earth resources satellite was launched 450 miles above Earth. As it passed over the Turkish-Russian border it recorded a mysterious boat-like object on Mt. Ararat.

Where did this mysterious ship come from?

Who put it there?

What was its cargo?

IN SEARCH OF NOAH'S ARK

by

Dave Balsiger & Charles E. Sellier Jr.

Sun Classic Books

CONTENTS

The 5,000-Year-Old Mystery

Courts of law deal with mysteries all the time. They solve mysteries by sorting out the true facts from the alleged facts. And a jury makes its decision based upon the facts presented by both sides during the trial.

This book presents a number of facts about an artifact on a mountaintop in Eastern Turkey. You are in the jury box; you can decide the case.

Your verdict will be important—because this book examines a mystery that has perplexed civilizations for approximately 5,000 years. The mystery has influenced all civilizations of the world, has claimed the lives of explorers, and, within the past ten years, has been the subject of CIA interests and Soviet KGB investigations.

If this mysterious artifact has created such international interest, why hasn't the scientific community investigated it and provided the world with massive volumes of conclusions?

The answer appears to be a matter of priorities. Scientists are preoccupied with more commercial endeavors—such as developing faster transportation or curing cancer. It would be very difficult to raise money to investigate an artifact located on a mountain in Turkey, and the outcome of the research probably would not solve man's current pressing needs.

There are, however, a small number of scientists who have set aside all these negative reasons and are diligently working to find a solution to this mystery—to identify the origin of this artifact. Undoubtedly, it will be another five or ten years before major scientific organizations acknowledge the evidence we will reveal here. Therefore, it is up to you to act as our jury and ultimate judge.

In a court of law, there is a term called "the undisputed facts." These are the facts that can be agreed to by those on either side of an issue.

The Undisputed Facts

Let's start our inquiry by looking at those facts which are undisputed in this mystery.

1. At about the 14,000 foot level on Mt. Ararat in Turkey, there is a very large wooden boat-like structure buried beneath many feet of ice and snow.

2. A boat-like structure has been mentioned as being on Mt. Ararat by explorers and historians of several civilizations beginning as early as 700 B.C.

3. During the 1800's, this structure was observed by many local explorers including numerous Turkish military authorities who gave the structure official governmental recognition in the news media.

4. In 1955, a filmed expedition recovered wood from the structure nearly 35 feet below the surface of an ice pack.

5. The recovered wood, subjected to numerous types of dating tests, revealed an age range of from 1,200 to 5,000 years old.

6. Early in the decade of the 70's, American spy planes, weather and military satellites photographed the structure on Mt. Ararat.

7. The only specific historical source that can be used to possibly identify this artifact is found in the Biblical book of Genesis which mentions the ancient landing of a large boat "on the mountains of Ararat."

2

Those are the undisputed facts. From here we will present the evidence to you, our jury. You will have the opportunity to examine all of the events, view the photographs, read the documents and determine the verdict— what is that artifact on the mountaintop in Eastern Turkey?

Is it Noah's Ark or some other large boat? If it is not Noah's Ark, how did it get there? Who put it there, and why?

We are sure you will be just as intrigued as we were in attempting to put this puzzle together and draw a conclusion.

CHAPTER 1

Is the Bible a Historically Reliable Document?

There is definitely a mysterious artifact on Mt. Ararat! But could it really be the Biblical Ark? This story has left its impact on us. Our society is filled with modern day versions of the Noah's Ark story. Toys, games and cartoons surround us.

Today more than one and a half billion people—Christians, Jews and Moslems—know the story of Noah's Ark surviving the Great Flood. The story is taught to us as children; it's a story enjoyed by people of all ages and a story so moving and powerful that it has survived nearly 5,000 years.

For all those years the story has been generally accepted as fact. But during the last century, with the advent of aggressive scientific inquiry, skeptics have come forth to label the story dubious—a combination of fact and fancy. They have said the Biblical story of Noah and the Flood is nothing more than legend.

Yet something must have occurred to have half of the earth's population still talking about such an event 5,000 years later. As a matter of fact, the report of a universal flood is found in more than 200 different cultural accounts of ancient and present civilizations.

Cultural accounts from almost every distant corner of the world record the occurrence of a great flood. Stories telling of this catastrophe range from the Australian aborigines to the Egyptians, from the Eskimos to South American Fuegians, and to the most famous source of them all—the Bible.

But can we rely on the Bible to have reported accurately on such an event as the Great Flood?

Archaeology Digs Up The Past

One of the newer sciences is archaeology. Civilizations left by men who lived thousands of years ago have been recovered carefully and laboriously as archaeologists have delved beneath the surface of the Earth.

They have excavated at hundreds of sites that through the ages had seemed nothing more than barren hills. But modern man has found that these "tells"—as they are called—often contain the ruins of past civilizations. They have been built up, layer by layer, level upon level, strata upon strata, as a civilization has been developed, destroyed, abandoned, and then begun again.

So it happens that through thousands of years, a considerable amount of archaeological evidence proving the historical accuracy of the Bible has been perfectly sealed, waiting for the science of archaeology to develop in the middle years of the 19th century.

But even earlier, in the year 1798, Napoleon was to play a part in the coming birth of Biblical archaeology. In that year, Napoleon with 328 vessels and 38,000 men left Paris on his conquest of Egypt.

From a military viewpoint, Napoleon's raid into Egypt was ill-advised. He held the land for only a year. But there was one incident that was to have a greater long range impact on the world than anyone could have imagined at the time.

This was the amazing discovery made at Rosetta, near the mouth of the Nile River. Napoleon had taken with him 120 scholars and artists whose duty it was to search out the land of Egypt. At Rosetta, they came across the now famous Rosetta Stone.

The discovery of this black basalt slab in 1798 marked the earliest beginnings of Biblical archaeology. For the decipherment of its three languages—the hieroglyphics (the system of writing used in ancient Egypt) Demotic (the simplified form of ancient Egyptian writing) and Greek—provided the key for unlocking the secrets of the past in this mysterious land of the Nile. The message of this stone, written in each of the three languages, was a decree by Priests of Memphis (the capital of ancient Egypt) honoring Ptolemy V (203-181 B.C.).

It has been said by many scientists that the deciphering of the Rosetta Stone was more significant than all the inventions of Thomas Edison. It unlocked the ancient languages of many lost and forgotten civilizations, several of which were mentioned by the Biblical writers. With the decipherment came the restoration of faith in the Bible as a historically reliable document.

Almost every day something new in archaeology is discovered that sheds additional light on the stories of the Bible. During the past 50 years, more books have been written on Biblical archaeology than on any other aspect of archaeology. Today, lining the shelves of major libraries, we find Bible dictionaries, Biblical encyclopedias, Bible atlases and dozens of other scholarly volumes. Collectively, these Biblical resource volumes give us more minute detail about numerous ancient civilizations of the early world than any other group of published books.

Archaeology Supports Genesis

Let's look at the archaeological evidence which proves the historical accuracy of passages in the Biblical book of Genesis—the same book where we find the account of Noah.

Gen. 1.1 through 2:25 tells the story of creation. The "Creation Tablets", found in ancient Nineveh between 1848 and 1876 in the excavated library of the Assyrian King Ashurbanipal (669-627 B.C.), record a similar version of creation in cuneiform writing on seven clay tablets. The tablets, which are considered historical documents, were made earlier in the reign of Hammurabi (1728-1686 B.C.), nearly 200 years before Moses wrote the book of Genesis.

To the layman, inscribed stones or clay tablets may not appear as spectacular as the ruins of ancient cities and buried treasure. To the archaeologist, and for the purposes of illumination of Biblical accounts or verification of

7

the Bible's historical accuracy, they may be even more important.

An example of such a stone tablet is the Sinaitic Inscription, one of the most important inscriptions ever found and one of the prized objects in the Cairo Museum. It was discovered in 1906 on the Sinai Peninsula, about 20 miles east of the Red Sea. Until this time, most scholars questioned whether Moses could actually have written the first five books of the Bible.

The reason for their disbelief is that an alphabetic script did not exist at that early time. But this inscribed stone tablet is indeed an alphabetic script, and all scholars agree that it dates back to at least the year 1600 B.C. It would have been difficult for Moses to use the Egyptian hieroglyphic language with its 750 common figures and 3,500 not so common figures. But the alphabetic script was in use at least 150 years before he needed it.

The Garden of Eden was part of that Genesis creation account. Eden was located in the lower Tigris-Euphrates Valley. Archaeologists and historians have confirmed that this valley was indeed the cradle of civilization.

In Gen. 4:22, it says Lamech's (one of the pre-flood patriarchs) wife, Zillah, gave birth to Tubal-cain, who became the father of metal workers in bronze and iron. For a long time historians placed the bronze and iron ages at more recent dates noting that the earlier Biblical timetable must be in error.

Then archaeologists discovered that copper existed as early as 4500 B.C. and that by 3000 B.C. it displaced stone for tools and weapons. An iron dagger handle existed in Tell Asmar in the century 2700 B.C.

Written Records of Flood

Now let's examine, briefly, some ancient historical records relating to the Flood. Both Sumerian and Babylonian clay tablets used to record history show that the Flood occurred.

The Sumerian tablets from the Nippur excavation along

the Euphrates River, dating before 2000 B.C., is the oldest account. The Babylonian account in cuneiform writing is found in the 11th book of the Gilgamesh Epic, which we will discuss in Chapter 2.

Archaeologist H. Rassam unearthed the Gilgamesh tablets at Nineveh (ancient capital of Assyria) from Ashurbanipal's royal library. These provide the most striking extra-Biblical parallel to Biblical events, including the account of the Babylonian Noah sending out birds from a ship.

Genesis Tells of Ziggurats

The table of nations, recorded in Gen. 10:1-32, has been illuminated and clarified by modern archaeology. This table tells which of Noah's sons and grandsons and great grandsons ruled where. It thus reflects the geopolitical state of the world at that time, including who ruled in such far-off places as Spain and Africa.

The descendants of Japheth formed the northern nations—Indo-European countries including Turkey and the southeastern part of the Soviet Union. Ham's descendants formed the southern nations and were among the earliest empire builders in southern Babylonia and Egypt. Shem's descendants made up the central nations known today as Saudi Arabia, Iraq and Iran.

Genesis 11:1-9 mentions the building of the Tower of Babel . . . or Babylon . . . in a city that thrived as a capital of the world. It was the first such tower attempted, and a symbol of man's revolt and rebellion against God, according to the Genesis account. Archaeologists have struggled long to find the tower which they now believe is in the Mesopotamian Valley near ancient Babylon. They have found evidence of a large tower, a multi-storied, stepped pyramid called a "ziggurat." The tower, made of sun-dried bricks, housed the city's patron deity in a shrine on the top story.

Ur, Abraham's birthplace, has become one of the best known ancient sites of southern Babylonia (Iraq) since Sir Leonard Woolley's excavations of 1922-34.

Abraham left the city during the third Babylonian dynasty (2070-1960 B.C.) when Ur was at the height of its splendor as a cult center dedicated to the moon-god Nanna and at the peak of its commercial prosperity. He first settled in Haran, an ancient city in southern Turkey, and later moved on to Canaan, known as Israel today.

In Gen. 12:10-20 Abraham and his family moved to Egypt to escape famine in Canaan. He was later kicked out of Egypt under armed escort for lying to the Pharaoh about his wife. The visit was made during the Middle Kingdom under Dynasty XII (1989-1776 B.C.). Archaeologists have discovered Egyptian tomb monuments showing bands of Semitic traders entering Egypt at such early times, illustrating Abraham's visit.

When Abraham was in Egypt, he no doubt saw the 190 foot high "step pyramid" at Saggara and must have heard of the Great Pyramid of Khufu, which was built a century before his visit.

The Khufu pyramid towers about 500 feet into the sky. Each side of its base is a staggering 756 feet long. Each stone—and there are 2,300,000 of them—weighs 2½ tons. Historians estimate that it took 100,000 men 30 years to construct the pyramid.

Sodom and Gomorrah, according to Gen. 19:1-32, were destroyed by God because of the gross wickedness of their inhabitants. The cities were in the Vale of Siddim at the southern end of the Dead Sea. This region, now covered with water, was fertile and populous in 2065 B.C. About 2050 B.C. in that area, a violent explosion hurled red-hot salt and free sulphur into the air, literally raining fire and brimstone over the plain. The ruins of Sodom and Gomorrah were still visible until the first century A.D.

There is a five-mile-long salt mass at the southwest end of the Dead Sea, called Jebel Usdum or "Mountain of Sodom." It lends credibility to the story of Lot's wife who was turned to salt during the catastrophe.

Patriarchal customs, described in Gen. 15:1 through 50:26 also are confirmed by archaeology. Such customs as adoption, marriage, rights of the first-born and others

10

are illustrated in the tablets from Nuzi, a Horite settlement discovered between 1925 and 1941, near Kirkuk in Iraq.

The Code of Hammurabi from 1700 B.C., discovered in 1901, and the Mari Letters from Tell el Hariri on the Middle Euphrates, discovered in 1933, also illustrate this patriarchal period written about by Moses in Genesis.

And in the Valley of the Inscriptions, heiroglyphs carved on the walls of the mountain caves more than 2,000 years ago tell of the nomadic wanderings of Biblical patriarchs.

Gen. 13:18 says Abram (later called Abraham) moved to Mamre near Hebron, the hill country of Judah in present day Israel. It was here that God warned Abraham of the destruction of Sodom and Gomorrah. Archaeologists have discovered Abraham's tomb in Hebron, confirming anew the drama of his life, the saga as it was told in Genesis.

The Bible alludes to an empire that for a very long time archaeologists could not prove existed. But in 1906 a German scientist, Hugo Winckler, uncovered tablets in central Turkey that confirmed the existence of the Hittite empire. The Hittite nation was one of several that God said would be conquered by Abraham's descendants as they invaded the promised land after the exodus from Egypt. (Gen. 14:13-18).[1]

Other Confirmations

Archaeology not only authenticates Genesis, but hundreds of other Bible passages.

We've learned that King Solomon's mines did exist. They are still open for tourists in the Holy Land to visit, at the edge of Sinai alongside the Red Sea, the site of Moses' crossing out of Egypt.

We now have archaeological proof of such cities as Megiddo, in Northern Israel, and Masada, by the Dead Sea in Israel. Megiddo was a fortified city where the pass across Mt. Carmel enters the Plain of Megiddo. It's mentioned in the Biblical books of Joshua, Judges and I Kings. Masada was the fortified desert retreat of Herod the Great. According to historian Josephus, it was also the place where John the Baptist was put to death.

The ruins of Qumran stand near the Dead Sea. Not far above the ancient city are the caves where the Dead Sea Scrolls were found in 1947, further unlocking the mysteries of the Bible.

Dr. Clifford Wilson, former director of the Australian Institute of Archaeology, points out other archaeological verifications of the Bible.

"Archaeologists take the Bible seriously," he says. "They have found that their archaeology touches Bible history. There's remarkable agreement, provided we recognize that the ancient historians are writing from their own point of view."[2]

Dr. Wilson cites papyri records found at the turn of the century that authenticate the Bible.

"These documents have shown that the New Testament records also must be taken very seriously as historical documents written in the everyday language of New Testament times," he says.

"Even details of the census, where people were ordered to return to their ancestral homes, have been found. That census is referred to in the Bible as the time when Jesus was born."

Significance of Dead Sea Scrolls

The Dead Sea Scrolls also have played their part. These sensational findings have demonstrated that the Old Testament documents already in existence have been remarkably preserved and transmitted through the long centuries to modern times.

No Hebrew copies of Old Testament documents were known, and these Scrolls date back about 1,000 years earlier than the earliest existing Hebrew documents known before this time, Dr. Wilson says.

The scrolls remained hidden in the almost inaccessible cliffs not far above the ancient city of Qumran, near the

Dead Sea, for centuries. But now their secrets have come to light, and fragments of every Old Testament book except Esther have been found. The scrolls also have thrown a great deal of light on the background of the New Testament.

The scrolls were found in several caves. One cave alone (No. 4) contained more than 10,000 fragments, representing about 380 manuscripts.

"They were not all Jewish Scriptures," Dr. Wilson concedes, "for this was part of a general library of their national literature.

"There was, of course, a great amount of literary activity in the period between the Old and New Testaments, and fragments of some of those non-Biblical writings are included in the Dead Sea Scrolls."

One of the most important scrolls found, in Cave No. 1, was a complete copy of Isaiah's prophecy telling of the coming of Jesus Christ. It is now generally accepted that this Isaiah Scroll dates to about 150 B.C.—well before the time of Christ, Dr. Wilson says.

Early Use Of Camels Confirmed

It once was thought that camels had not been domesticated by Abraham's time. While it is true they were used more widely from the time of Solomon onwards, camels were at times used long before Abraham moved around the lands of the Bible.

There are several references in the Book of Genesis to camels. Abraham and other patriarchs used them (Gen. 12:16, 24:10, etc.).

It has been said that no camels existed in Palestine in patriarchal times. However, bones and teeth of camels have been recovered there. One figurine in Egypt dating to about 3000 B.C. shows a man beside his kneeling camel. And another figurine from Lagash in Mesopotamia dates to about 2350 B.C.

"Scholars at one time suggested that when the Bible writers referred to Abraham's camels, they actually meant

13

asses, and that this was an anachronism—something written up at a later time, using a later setting to describe the earlier happening," Dr. Wilson says. "The references to camels were supposed to be strong evidence for the later writing of these stories, for it was argued that they were put in writing when camels had replaced donkeys. Now the Bible word has been shown to be correct after all."

Lions, too, are of interest archaeologically. In the book of Nahum 2:11-13, we read, "Where is the dwelling place of the lions?" In the Book of Daniel we read how Daniel was cast into a den of lions.

Until recently no one quite knew what the prophet Nahum was referring to. Why was he talking about lions? Today, archaeological evidence indicates that Nahum was referring to the caged lions in Nineveh against which he pronounced the judgment of God.

Many scenes of the lion hunt are depicted on the walls of ancient palaces, such as at Nineveh on the palace walls of the famous Assyrian king Ashurbanipal. The king is shown setting off for the hunt, and he is seen in hand to paw combat with a lion. Further along the palace wall, he is depicted pouring a libation over four lions at the royal temple.

"Where is the dwelling place of lions?" Nahum asked. What did he mean? He was saying that the very center so important to the sport of kings, the capital itself, would be destroyed. It was destroyed in 612 B.C. by combined onslaughts of the Babylonians and Medes.

The idea of Daniel being cast into the lions' den seemed wrong to Bible critics. It wasn't known that there were lions in Babylon; they certainly were not native to the area.

However, a black basalt statue of a lion has been found at Babylon, that dates back to the days of Daniel. Though lions were not native to Assyria and Babylonia, they were imported especially for the ancient sport of kings.

Again, the Bible background is quite accurate.

Shrines to Diana Support

The silver shrines of Diana are another archaeological support of the Bible.

The Apostle Paul lived for three years in Ephesus, from A.D. 50-54, against a background of religious superstition. In Acts 19 of the New Testament, we read of a near-riot when Paul continued to preach that Jesus was the true God.

"Demetrius the silversmith was engaged in the manufacture of images of the goddess Diana," Dr. Wilson explains. "He stirred up his fellow craftsmen, claiming that Paul was turning the people away from the worship of Diana whom 'all Asia and the world worships.'

"A great crowd had gathered, and at Demetrius' urging they cried out, 'Great is Diana of the Ephesians' (Acts 19:28).

"The image of the goddess was supposed to have fallen from Heaven, and to have been set up in her temple at Ephesus," says Dr. Wilson.

In *Luke the Historian*, Dr. J. A. Thompson comments on the temple:

Excavations at Ephesus have revealed the remains of the temple Diana. Its dimensions were 160 feet by 340 feet. The ancient altar was found to be 20 feet square. The divine statue probably stood closest to this. Many fragments of large white marble tiles which covered the roof, and parts of fluted columns were found. Over 700 inscriptions were brought to light.

The great temple was built on marshy soil. Today the site is a stagnant pool, permanently flooded. An idea of the external appearance and magnificence of the temple is found from Roman coins.

Dr. Thompson also says the gold and silver images of the goddess Artemis (the Greek Diana) found in the theater at Ephesus, weighed between three and seven pounds, and the custom was for them to be presented to

15

the goddess and then placed in her temple. A special endowment paid for the upkeep of the images.

In the temple itself, Thompson says, dating to as early as the eighth century B.C., more than 2,000 gifts dedicated to Artemis were recovered. There also were about 5,000 ornamental objects, together with earrings, brooches, coins and necklaces.

"It is clear that the worship of Diana, as she was known in Paul's day, was a lucrative business for various craftsmen," Dr. Wilson says.

There also is mention of the theater at Ephesus: "And the whole city was filled with confusion: and having caught Gaius and Aristarchus, men of Macedonia, Paul's companions in travel, they rushed with one accord into the theater" (Acts 19:29).

This renowned theater can still be seen. It was almost 500 feet in diameter and would have held nearly 25,000 people!

Bible Accurate

From the foregoing evidence, we've seen that the Bible (especially the book of Genesis) is a remarkable historical document as well as an archaeologically accurate source book. It has resulted in thousands of archaeological finds and scores of scholarly volumes about ancient civilizations.

The Bible, which has proved to be accurate wherever it can be checked out and has stood the test in little matters and in great happenings, has also told about a flood—a world-wide flood and a man along with his family who were saved from that flood because of their Ark.

It is reasonable to assume that the same standard of Biblical accuracy—proven by the evidence of archaeological finds—would have been maintained in the reporting of the Flood and of Noah's Ark. This hypothesis being true, researchers should be able to correlate the Biblical flood account with other historical documents or cultural traditions indicating that a flood did actually occur.

Footnotes
Chapter 1

1. Unger, Merrill F., *Unger's Bible Handbook,* (Moody Press, Chicago, IL, 1966), pp. 18-69.
2. Statements made during a February, 1976 interview. Dr. Clifford Wilson is Senior Professor of Archaeology at Monash University in Melbourne, Australia.

CHAPTER 2

Is a Great Flood Supported by Cultural History?

In our quest for evidence about the unidentified artifact, let's now look at the section of the Bible where Noah's story is told. What is the real story of the Flood? Who actually built the Ark, and why was it built? What does the Bible really say about the Ark's landing site?

Noah's Story

The story of Noah in the Bible begins with God's dissatisfaction with the world He had created. The Bible says God looked upon the world's corruption and violence and vowed to destroy the Earth and all those in it because of man's sinfulness.

But there was one man living then that found grace in the eyes of the Lord. He was Noah, a just man who walked with God.

Noah, his wife, three sons and their wives are believed by most scholars to have lived in the fertile crescent of the Mesopotamian Valley, between the Tigris and Euphrates Rivers—a part of the Middle East now known as Iraq.

We know very little about Noah, except that he and his sons, Shem, Ham and Japheth, were men of faith who resisted all the sinfulness and corruption of their day.

Noah's story is recorded in Genesis 6:1 through 9:29. We quote directly from *The New American Bible,* Catholic version, beginning with Genesis 6:12.

When God saw how corrupt the earth had become, since all mortals led depraved lives on earth, he said to

18

Noah: "I have decided to put an end to all mortals on earth; the earth is full of lawlessness because of them. So I will destroy them and all life on earth.

Preparation for the Flood

"Make yourself an ark of gopherwood, put various compartments in it, and cover it inside and out with pitch.

"This is how you shall build it: the length of the ark shall be three hundred cubits, its width fifty cubits, and its height thirty cubits.

"Make an opening for daylight in the ark, and finish the ark a cubit above it. Put an entrance in the side of the ark, which you shall make with bottom, second and third decks.

"I, on my part, am about to bring the flood (waters) on the earth, to destroy everywhere all creatures in which there is breath of life; everything on earth shall perish.

"But with you I will establish my covenant; you and your sons, your wife and your sons' wives, shall go into the ark.

"Of all other living creatures you shall bring two into the ark, one male and one female, that you may keep them alive with you. . . .

"Moreover you are to provide yourself with all the food that is to be eaten, and store it away, that it may serve as provisions for you and for them."

This Noah did; he carried out all the commands that God gave him.

The Bible says God gave Noah the flood destruction warning 125 years ahead of the actual event. During this time Noah no doubt preached of the coming destruction and spent an undisclosed number of years building the Ark while waiting for God's next instruction which came on the completion of the Ark. The new instructions were more specific concerning the animals and the exact timing of the flood. Our account resumes with Genesis 7:1.

Then the Lord said to Noah: "Go into the ark, you and all your household, for you alone in this age have I found to be truly just.

"Of every clean animal, take with you seven pairs, a male and its mate; and of the unclean animals, one pair, a male and its mate; likewise, of every clean bird of the air, seven pairs, a male and female, and of all the unclean birds, one pair, a male and female. . . .

"Seven days from now I will bring rain down on the earth for forty days and forty nights, and so I will wipe out from the surface of the earth every moving creature that I have made. . . ."

The Great Flood

Of the clean animals and the unclean, of the birds, and of everything that creeps on the ground, male and female entered the ark with Noah, just as the Lord had commanded him.

As soon as the seven days were over, the waters of the flood came upon the earth.

In the six hundredth year of Noah's life, in the second month, on the seventeenth day of the month: it was on that day that all the fountains of the great abyss burst forth, and the floodgates of the sky were opened. . . .

The flood continued upon the earth for forty days. As the waters increased, they lifted the ark, so that it rose above the earth.

The swelling waters increased greatly, but the ark floated on the surface of the waters.

Higher and higher above the earth rose the waters until all the highest mountains everywhere were submerged, the crest rising fifteen cubits higher than the submerged mountains.

All creatures that stirred on earth perished; birds, cattle, wild animals, and all that swarmed on the earth, as well as all mankind. . . . Only Noah and those with him in the ark were left.

The waters maintained their crest over the earth for one hundred and fifty days.

The Waters Subside

But God remembered Noah and all the animals, wild and tame, that were with him in the ark. So God made a wind sweep over the earth, and the waters began to subside.

The fountains of the abyss and the floodgates of the sky were closed, and the downpour from the sky was held back.

Gradually, the waters receded from the earth. At the end of one hundred and fifty days, the waters had so diminished that, in the seventh month, on the seventeenth day of the month, the ark came to rest on the mountains of Ararat.

The waters continued to diminish until the tenth month, and on the first day of the tenth month the tops of the mountains appeared.

The Birds Go Forth

At the end of forty days Noah opened the hatch he had made in the ark, and he sent out a raven, to see if the waters had lessened on the earth. It flew back and forth until the waters dried off from the earth.

Then he sent out a dove, to see if the waters had lessened on the earth.

But the dove could find no place to alight and perch, and it returned to him in the ark. . . .

He waited seven days more and again sent the dove out from the ark.

In the evening the dove came back to him, and there in its bill was a plucked-off olive leaf! So Noah knew that the waters had lessened on the earth.

He waited still another seven days and then released the dove once more; and this time it did not come back.

In the six hundred and first year of Noah's life, in the first month, on the first day of the month, the water began to dry up on the earth. Noah then removed the covering of the ark and saw that the surface of the ground was drying up.

In the second month, on the twenty-seventh day of the month, the earth was dry.

The Ark is Emptied

Then God said to Noah: "Go out of the ark, together with your wife and your sons and your sons' wives.

"Bring out with you every living thing that is with you—all bodily creatures, be they birds or animals or creeping things of the earth—and let them abound on the earth, breeding and multiplying on it."

So Noah came out, together with his wife and his sons and his sons' wives; and all the animals. . . .

Then Noah built an altar to the Lord, and . . . offered holocausts (burnt offerings) on the altar.

When the Lord smelled the sweet odor, he said to himself: "Never again will I doom the earth because of man since the desires of man's heart are evil from the start; nor will I ever again strike down all living beings, as I have done.

"As long as the earth lasts seedtime and harvest, cold and heat, summer and winter, and day and night shall not cease."

Covenant With Noah

God blessed Noah and his sons and said to them: "Be fertile and multiply and fill the earth. [Reproduction of the Earth is where a lot of Bible critics find fault with the story of Noah. These problems will be discussed in Chapter 9.]

"Dread fear of you shall come upon all the animals of the earth and all the birds of the air, upon all the creatures that move about on the ground and all the fishes of the sea; into your power they are delivered. . . . [Prior to the Flood, animals apparently did not fear man—a subject which will be discussed in Chapter 9.]

God said to Noah and to his sons with him: "See, I am now establishing my covenant with you and your descendants after you and with every living creature that was with you. . . .

"I will establish my covenant with you that never again shall all bodily creatures be destroyed by the waters of a flood; there shall not be another flood to devastate the earth."

God added: "This is the sign that I am giving for all

ages to come, of the covenant between me and you and every living creature with you: I set my bow (rainbow) in the clouds to serve as a sign of the covenant between me and the earth. . . ."

Noah lived three hundred and fifty years after the flood. The whole lifetime of Noah was nine hundred and fifty years; then he died.

So ends the story of Noah, according to the Bible.

Is Noah's Story True?

Is it legend, Biblical folklore, a dubious combination of fact and fancy? Or is it true?

Could the Ark have been built so that it would have stayed afloat for almost 13 months? Would it have been big enough to carry all those animals? Was it stable enough to ride out the storms and subterranean upheavals that churned the waters? More importantly, was the Earth really covered with water?

Valid questions! Now let's examine the evidence. . .

Flood Would Cause Memorable Impact

A great deluge, which destroyed all the life on Earth except for those aboard the Ark, would not be quickly forgotten, like the headlines of yesterday's newspaper. One day the world existed with people, plants, and animals. Then a few days later, because of a great flood, all are gone. This was a catastrophe that affected all mankind. Surely such a destructive universal flood would have been recorded elsewhere besides the Bible. Let's see if other historical documents or cultural accounts support the theory of a great flood.

The Genesis Flood was bound to have had a traumatic effect on the survivors—Noah, his three sons and their wives.

And aside from the basic facts and observations of the catastrophe, each survivor no doubt injected his or her own feelings into the story as they told and retold it to

23

succeeding generations as Noah's sons and wives and descendants repopulated the world.

The story, which has survived about 5,000 years, can be found in some form in more than 200 different cultural accounts of past and present civilizations.

These accounts of a universal flood are truly global with one exception: the African accounts are limited to the Egyptians of North Africa.

Stories of the flood are found in the far reaches of the north, among the Eskimos of North America, the Siberian peoples of the Soviet Union, and the peoples of Finland and Iceland. To the south, we discover similar accounts among the Maori of New Zealand, the Australian aborigines, and the Tierra del Feugo natives at the tip of South America. Many of the accounts are recorded in anthropological records of past civilizations; others are simply passed on by word of mouth from generation to generation.

Dr. Arthur C. Custance, a student of cuneiform and Middle Eastern languages, is probably the world's only living expert who has studied the massive amount of cultural accounts relating to the Flood. He is a fellow of the Canadian Royal Anthropological Institute and has authored 52 treatises relating to ancient history, anthropology, archaeology, Biblical history and philosophy.

According to his essay on the "Flood Traditions of the World,"[1] the various accounts often differ widely from the Biblical record.

"However," says Dr. Custance, "they are in accord *both with it* and *among themselves* on the following four basic issues:

> "*1*. The cause was a 'moral' one. Man brought the Flood on himself either by his disobedience or because of lack of piety and reverence. In all the Flood accounts, with the one notable exception—the Flood tradition from Egypt—the catastrophe comes as a judgment.
>
> "2. They speak of one man who is warned of the coming catastrophe and thus saves not only him-

24

self but also his family or his friends. Forewarning is always given in some way. In the Biblical account, Noah is warned by revelation in a manner which is clear and reasonable if we allow that God is able to communicate with man.

"*3*. The world was depopulated except for these few survivors, from whom the present people of the world were derived. None of the flood accounts leaves one with the impression that the survivors named subsequently met any other survivors to form a new community for the repopulating of the area. They alone escaped in every case creating strong evidence for a universal flood rather than a local flood.

"*4*. Animals play a part either in conveying the warning, in providing the transportation to safety, or in giving information about the state of things after the Flood had subsided. Very frequently birds are mentioned in the accounts. The use of birds in antiquity and in modern times as navigational aids has been very widespread."[2]

Also the following features are often dealt with in one way or another lending further authenticity to the Biblical account, according to Dr. Custance.

1. In extra-Biblical accounts, the survivors always land on a local mountain. In the Hebrew account, the Ark lands far from Palestine in a distant country of which most Hebrew people had no firsthand knowledge.

This is an unusual circumstance because all other Flood accounts report that the Ark landed locally. In Greece, on Mount Parnassus;[3] in India, in the Himalayas;[4] and in America, one ancient Indian account has it landing on Keddie Peak in the Sacramento Valley.[5] Everywhere the same—always a local mountain.

"This circumstance surely suggests that here in the Bible we have the genuine account. And it also underscores the great respect that the Hebrew people had for the Word of God and the requirement that they never tamper with it. It would surely, otherwise, have been most natural for them to land the Ark on their most famous mountain, Mount Zion," says Dr. Custance.[6]

> *2.* Some of these accounts agree with the Bible in stating that eight souls survived.
>
> *3.* A number of the cultural accounts give extraordinarily graphic details of just such incidental circumstances as must have accompanied the event.
> In the various versions of the cuneiform accounts are embellishments which Noah's matter-of-fact account did not see fit to include, although the events very well may have been experienced by Noah or his family. For example, one cuneiform account tells of bodies floating about like logs in the water.[7]
>
> *4.* A small number of the accounts are almost certainly borrowed from Christian missionaries, but not nearly to the extent sometimes claimed.

"The great majority of these flood accounts have in common, as we have seen, only four basic elements. All other details—the nature of the warning, the escape "vessel," the part played by animals, and so forth—differ in such a way that borrowing from the Biblical record is virtually excluded altogether," says Dr. Custance.

"These native traditions of the flood are undoubtedly recollections from the very distant past of an event which was so stupendous that it was never forgotten, even though the details themselves became blurred, with local coloring restoring what had faded.

"In a sense, therefore, all these stories are in agreement, though in fact, they are often as different in detail as it is possible to imagine," explains Dr. Custance. "In a court of law the testimony of witnesses who both agree and disagree in this fashion is considered to be a more

26

powerful witness to the central truth than would be complete concord, for in the nature of the case collaboration is manifestly excluded."[8]

Now let's examine some of these cuneiform accounts to see how the historical writers of these clay tablets actually viewed the Flood.

During the reign of Assyrian king Ashurbanipal (669-627 B.C.), much attention was paid to the records associated with ancient buildings, libraries, and foundation structures. But this recording of historical data was short lived and on the death of King Ashurbanipal in 627 B.C., his library in Nineveh containing 100,000 clay tablets was sealed and forgotten until uncovered in the 1850's by a team of British archaeologists.

Gilgamesh Tablets Tell Noah's Story

King Ashurbanipal himself mentions a great flood. He wrote on one clay tablet, "I have read the artistic script of Sumer on the back of Akkadian, which is hard to master. Now I take pleasure in the reading of the stones coming from before the flood."[9]

This Assyrian king refers to the stones that came from before the flood. He knew that a great flood had covered the Earth, and among the thousands of tablets in his Royal library was the Epic of Gilgamesh.

When the excavators first found the Gilgamesh flood account at Nineveh, it was not complete. In 1873 a British newspaper sent George Smith, who had been employed at the British Museum, to Nineveh in Iraq to find the rest of the missing tablets. "It was an impossible assignment, but the amazing fact is that George Smith found the missing fragments," says Dr. Clifford Wilson.

Versions of the flood tablet have since been found in other places. One early record that combined both the flood and the creation account was the Epic of Atrahasis. This historical tablet was released to the world during the 1960's.

But still the most famous of these accounts is the Gilgamesh Epic. Three of the Gilgamesh tablets relate the story of Noah's Ark and the Flood using different names and some changes in the details of the event.

The Gilgamesh Epic, written in Akkadian, belonged to the heritage of the great nations of the ancient East. The epic originated with the Sumerians, the people whose capital stood on the ancient site of Ur in present day Iraq.[10]

Most semitic scholars generally agree that the Gilgamesh Epic is older than the Genesis Flood account, penned by Moses around 1475 B.C.—about 1400 years after the time of the universal flood.

Here is a synopsis of the Epic:

To ensure his immortality, a man called Gilgamesh went on a long journey to find his ancestor Utnapishtim, who was supposed to possess the secrets of immortal life by favor of the gods.

After locating him, Gilgamesh pleaded, "Please tell me the Secret of Life," to which Utnapishtim responded with the story of the Flood. He told Gilgamesh that at one time in history, the gods had decided to destroy mankind by a flood. He had been warned by the true god Ea to prepare for the destruction.

He was to build a ship, the length of which to be equal to its width.

Ea explained that the flood was because mankind hated him and no longer wanted him to live with them.

So Utnapishtim began to build the ship.

"Help came from everywhere," Utnapishtim told Gilgamesh. "Children brought pitch, while the grown-ups brought other materials. Five days after Ea spoke to me, I laid the keel. I made the floor space one iku in size and the walls of the ship one hundred twenty cubits long. I designed it and divided the ship into six decks, giving it a total of seven stories.

"Then I looked at the ground plan and divided it into nine sections, after which I drove water stoppers into the holes. Next I gathered punting poles and stored up a supply of food. But that wasn't all: To make it water-proof, I poured six shar of pitch into the furnace and three shar of asphalt and three shar of oil. Besides this, it took a shar of oil to saturate the water stoppers and two shar of oil for the boatman. . . .

"On New Year's day, the ship was finished and it caused a great celebration. I washed my hands; the job of building the ship had been a hard one.

"Hurriedly I gathered all my silver and gold and stashed it on the ship, and after I had put all my relatives aboard, I took representatives of all living creatures in the field into the ship and also took the craftsman.

"And in the evening, the sender of the storm started the rains. I looked at it and became frightened. I walked into the ship and shut the door behind me, and told Pazur-Amurri, the navigator, to take good care of the ship.

"Early the next morning, the first shimmer of the day was obscured by an ominous black thundercloud, and while the gods Shullat and Hanish announced the tragedy to come, Irragal's force pulled out our mast, and Ninurta's anger breached the dikes. The flashing light of Anunnaki illuminated the thundering skies while the raging of Adad could be heard all over the heavens.

"Then—darkness. All light disappeared; the land shook and broke like a pot. A whole day long the tempest raged. Like a battle it covered the people, and no one could see his neighbor. Not even heaven could recognize the people. So awesome was the spectacle that even the gods became frightened and terror stricken. In confusion they fled and ascended to the heaven of Anu and there cowered like dogs. . . .

"And for six days and six nights the winds continued, and the rains kept coming down, and the flood that resulted covered the land, but on the seventh day of the terrible storm, the flood which had covered everything like a devouring army, grew quiet, and the storm stopped and the flood waters became quiet.

"I looked at the sea and everything was still ... and all the people had become dust.

"I went to the roof and opened a porthole and the sunlight touched my face and I bowed my head and sat down and cried—and the tears ran down my face.

"I looked at the horizon trying to find the end of the ocean, but it was not until 48 hours later that I saw the first sign of land. It was Mount Nisir, and when we reached it, it held us fast. It did not let us go again.

"Six long days the mountain held on to us and on the

seventh day I decided to let a dove go, but soon she returned to me, for she had not been able to find a resting place.

"And then I sent the raven, and when she saw that the waters were going down she flew around for a while, cawed and took off. After that I let all the birds go and offered a sacrifice.

"I took refreshments to the peak of the mountain in seven kettles, and used sweet cane, cedar, and myrtle for firewood, and when the gods smelled that they gathered like flies over the sacrifice."

After an exchange of anger and accusations between the gods, who came to observe the sacrifice, Ea took Utnapishtim and his wife into the ship and blessed them, saying:

"Up to this moment, Utnapishtim, you have been a mere mortal, but from now on both you and your wife will be like gods among us. From now on you will live in the far distance at the mouth of the rivers."

Utnapishtim concludes his narrative to Gilgamesh by saying, "And so I joined the gods, and they made me live among them at the mouth of the rivers."

Could Utnapishtim have been the Biblical Noah?

There are some striking similarities between the epic and the Biblical account. Merrill F. Unger in his third edition of *Archaeology and the Old Testament*, pages 55-65, points them out:

1. Both accounts state that the Flood was divinely planned.

2. Both agree that the impending catastrophe was divinely revealed to the hero of the Flood.

3. Both connect the Flood with the defection of the human race.

4. Both tell of the deliverance of the hero and his family.

5. Both assert that the hero was divinely instructed to build a huge boat to preserve life.

6. Both indicated the physical causes of the Deluge.

7. Both specify the duration of the Deluge, although they differ in the elapsed time.

8. Both name the landing place of the boat.

9. Each tells of sending birds at certain intervals to determine the decrease of waters.

10. Both describe acts of worship by the hero after his deliverance.

11. Both allude to special blessings upon the hero after the disaster.

Researcher Alfred M. Rehwinkel, in *The Flood,* page 162, notes a number of differences between the two stories. His conclusion is that though there are definite areas of agreement, these areas indicate that the two stories are based on the same event, not the same account.

Other Flood Accounts

The principal features of the Biblical record are apparent in a number of flood accounts from throughout the world. Except in the case of an Egyptian and one of two Scandinavian accounts, all traditions include destruction by flood. And the Egyptian and Scandinavian traditions record partial destruction by flood. In most of them, an ark is provided and human seed is saved.[11]

Chinese legends of the deluge are among the most striking found in Asia.

A flood of devastating force is said to have occurred around 2300 B.C. (although one account puts the date at 2297 B.C.). This flood, the story goes, was caused by an overflow of the great rivers and stopped by the swelling of the sea. The Chinese hero, Fah-Le, escaped the destruction with his wife and three children.[12]

Other traditions on mainland China say all Chinese are descendants of "Nu-wah", an ancient ancestor who distinguished himself by overcoming a great flood.

Dr. E. W. Thwing, a researcher who spent many years in China, has made a successful search into the probable connection between the Chinese story and the Genesis record.

He discovered that ancient Chinese writing has numerous words that can only be traced to "Nu-wah" and the Flood. The word used for "ship," for example, as printed in Chinese books and papers today, is an ancient character made up of the picture of a "boat" and "eight mouths." This shows that the first ship was a boat carrying eight people, Thwing says.

The Chinese characters for "Nu" (meaning *woman*) and "wah" (meaning *flowery*) were not used for their meaning, but for their sound. While the ancient one has been thought to be a female, the fact that the characters are used for their sound would indicate an ancient man, famous in a flood, the sound of whose name was kept as "Nu-wah."

Could the Chinese "Nu-wah" and the Biblical Noah be the same person?

Eskimos in Alaska tell the story of a flood accompanied by a simultaneous earthquake. Those who survived—and there were only a few—fled in canoes or took refuge on the highest peaks.

In America there are 58 different Indian deluge accounts. The Navajo Indians believed that the Grand Canyon was the result of the Great Flood.

Other Indian tribes believed that the flood was caused by the wrath of the underworld water monsters. The story goes on to explain how an Indian was saved from the flood by a raft this hero had built, and that the hero had taken animals aboard. The raft came to rest on a mountain peak after the flood waters receded.

The Indians believed all of the various flood accounts long before exposure to the Europeans and their Christian concepts of the Flood.

Fernand Navarra cites the flood Legend of Berose in *Noah's Ark: I Touched It*. Berose was a third century B.C. Chaldean priest.

The god Chronos appears to the tenth antediluvian king, Xisuthros (or Sisuthros), and announces that soon all men will perish in a deluge. He enjoins him to ... build a ship and take refuge there with his family and dearest friends. Xisuthros builds a ship, five stadia long and two stadia wide, fills it with food supplies and gets aboard with his family. . . .

The Deluge comes, engulfs the rest of mankind, then recedes. Xisuthros lets a few birds go, and they come back, having found no dry land. A few days later, he lets them go once more; they return with mud on their feet. Let loose a third time, they do not return.

Xisuthros then notices that his vessel has stopped on a mountain in Armenia.[18]

According to the story, the people of Berose's time could still see the remains of Xisuthros' ship on the Gordyan mountains (the ancient name of the area between Kurdistan and Lake Van) in the Ararat region.

Other Flood traditions appear in Europe, two main versions coming from Greek and Latin mythology; Asia, Africa, Central and South America and the islands of the sea.

Last Event Shared by All Men

The universality of the Flood tradition is apparent from all these accounts. The memory of mankind in every corner of the globe bears witness to the reality of a tremendous Deluge.

While all over the globe a tradition of the great Flood may be found, it appears that this is the last great event in which mankind shared. The Bible goes on to mention other amazing events. But none of these subsequent events are commonly found throughout the world as cherished traditions. It seems most unlikely that native people in different parts of the world would completely forget the Tower of Babel, the destruction of Sodom and Gomorrah, or the events of the Exodus from Egypt.

Why should they all remember only this single event— the Great Flood? It is reasonable to assume that it was indeed the final great event shared by mankind. The survivors spread abroad after coming out of the Ark and were not aware of these later, yet equally important, events.

"The measure of agreement between these stories in their essentials is some indication that the number of people who originally experienced this catastrophe and survived it was quite small—indeed, probably a single family," says Dr. Custance.[14]

There is little doubt that of the more than 200 known cultural flood accounts, the Biblical record is the only one that can really be accepted as an authentic *eyewitness* account. Sir William Dawson wrote on this subject years ago:

> I have long thought that the narrative in Genesis 7 and 8 can be understood only on the supposition that it is a contemporary journal or log of an eye-witness incorporated by the author of Genesis in his work.

> The dates of the rising and fall of the water, the note of soundings over the hilltops when the maximum was attained, and many other details as well as the whole tone of the narrative, seem to require this supposition. . . .[15]

There are in all of the other flood accounts elements introduced that could not have been witnessed by the survivors. This is true even of the cuneiform accounts mentioned earlier in this chapter.

Dr. Custance also believes from his research that Genesis is an eyewitness account of the flood. "To me it seems almost self-evident that once Noah and his family were inside the Ark and the rains began, from there on God's revelation has not entered into the account. Like any other good captain, Noah kept his daily journal, marking off the events of the days and the weeks and the months, carefully and precisely and accurately, as he and his crew experienced them."[16]

The cultural evidence that there was a great flood and a man who survived it is recorded anthropological history.

With the amount of anthropological evidence available

from every corner of the world indicating that a universal Deluge did occur, it should be possible for researchers to gather scientific data supporting a worldwide flood. Any destructive flood leaves behind telltale signs in the Earth's crust. But in what form are these signs after nearly 5,000 years? Will we be able to recognize them as results of a Deluge?

Footnotes
Chapter 2

1. Patten, Donald W., *A Symposium on Creation* (Baker Book House, Grand Rapids, MI, 1972), p. 9-10.
2. Hornell, James, "The Role of Birds in Early Navigation," *Antiquity*, Vol. 20, 1946, p. 145.
3. Nelson, Byron, *The Deluge Story in Stone* (Augsburg, Minneapolis, MN, 1931), p. 171.
4. Lord Arundell of Wardour, *Tradition: The Mythology and the Law of Nations* (Burns-Oats, London, 1872), p. 224.
5. Coon, C.S., *A Reader in General Anthropology* (Holt, New York, 1948), p. 281.
6. Patten, *op. cit.*, p. 17.
7. Barton, George, *Archaeology and the Bible* (American Sunday School Union, Philadelphia, PA, 1933), p. 337.
8. Patten, *op. cit.*, p. 20.
9. Statements made during a February 1976 interview. Dr. Clifford Wilson is Senior Professor of Archaeology at Monash University in Melbourne, Australia.
10. Keller, Werner, *The Bible as History* (Morrow Co., New York, 1956), p. 34.
11. Montgomery, John Warwick, *The Quest for Noah's Ark* (Bethany Fellowship, Minneapolis, MN, 1972), p. 30.
12. Navarra, Fernand, *Noah's Ark: I Touched It* (Logos International, Plainfield, N.J., 1974), p. 107.
13. *Ibid.*, pp. 99-100.
14. Patten, *op. cit.*, p. 21.
15. Dawson, Sir J. William, *The Story of the Earth and Man*, 6th ed. (London, 1880), p. 290.
16. Patten, *op. cit.*, p. 22.

CHAPTER 3

Is There Scientific Evidence of a Universal Flood?

There is the flash of lightning, the rumble of thunder, and we hear the splatter of rain falling on the roof of Noah's Ark. The rain falls gently at first, then harder. The yells of people to "let us in" are muffled by the falling rain. The rain becomes torrential; the roar of thunder and the crack of lightning is deafening.

We see the rain and wind tearing at the trees; a river overflows its banks and washes over the land. We see people running and screaming; water sweeps through the streets.

The Ark is abruptly lifted by the flooding waters as we see the rain pouring in solid sheets onto the flood waters. We can no longer see trees or mountains—only vistas of stormy flood waters and more falling rain.

This short visual drama may give us a feeling about the great Flood, but words cannot describe the powerful waves of flooding water that must have swept the planet with a swift and fierce force to have left such massive scars in the Earth's crust.

The Earth must have trembled and quaked, allowing subterranean waters to gush up through the surface to join the pelting rains.

Today many of our great mountains—the Andes, the Himalayas, the Rockies and the Alps—bear the scars.

As scholars and scientists have studied the Earth's surface during the past 200 years, several theories about the Flood have developed. These theories range from no flood to the universal flood. We'll examine four of these theories.[1]

The first is the *nihilistic* view, which doesn't accept the Biblical record. Those who hold this view deny a flood ever occurred as described in Genesis.

Another theory is that the Flood was merely a *tidal wave*. While accepting most of the details of the Bible, proponents say the water that covered the hills resulted from tidal waves, not a global flood.

Agreeing there was a great amount of water and that great upheavals were caused by the opening of subterranean fountains; conceding there was an upsurge of great mountains and a lowering of the Earth's surface, which created great oceans, they believe the rolling of the Earth's surface produced tidal waves.

Tidal waves rise, then recede. They could never have produced the permanent-like conditions described in the Biblical Flood where the water prevailed on the Earth for 150 days before it began to subside. However, tidal waves were no doubt experienced during the Genesis Flood due to earthquakes—but not a valid theory for keeping the Earth flooded for nearly a year!

A third view is the *local flood* theory introduced by John Pye Smith in 1839. He said the Flood was no more than a local inundation in the Mesopotamian Valley, possibly caused by a great overflow of the Euphrates or some other river in the Middle East.

Smith maintained that the deluge could not have been universal, and to hold the universal view amounted to subterfuge in supposing a stupendous miracle. He gave 60 pages of arguments against the universality of the Flood in the fifth edition of his famous work, *On the Relation Between the Holy Scriptures and Some Parts of Geological Science*, published posthumously in 1854.

The theory gained part of its logic from the argument that if there were no universal geological evidences of the Flood, there must not have been a universal deluge.

Strangely enough in Smith's day, the early 1800's, the geological sciences were not developed enough either to prove or disprove a local or universal flood. Yet his theory gained wide acceptance.

Local Flood Theory Doesn't Hold Water

The local flood theory became popular in the late 19th century and is held by some modern day scholars because of the Ur excavations done in Iraq around 1930.

Sir Leonard Woolley claimed in 1929 to have found conclusive evidence of the Flood in an eight-foot stratum of clean clay under the ancient city of Ur in the lower Mesopotamia. A few months afterward, Professor Stephen Langdon announced he had made a similar discovery at Kish, a few hundred miles north.

The discoveries rocked the world. The universal flood believers of the day viewed the evidence as conclusive proof that a great universal flood did occur. On the other hand, Sir Leonard and Professor Langdon viewed their finds as supporting the local flood theory.

The joy soon faded. The so-called flood deposits at Kish and Ur were not contemporaneous. And in fact, the flood at Ur only inundated part of the city. Neither did these flood deposits provide evidence of the universal flood.

G. Ernest Wright in *Biblical Archaeology,* page 119, says, "Woolley seems to have dug some five pits through the early strata of occupation at Ur, but in only two of them did he find deposits of water-borne debris. The logical inference from this is that the flood in question did not cover the whole city of Ur, but only part of it. Furthermore, the site showed no break in occupation as a result of the flood, which we should expect if there had been a major catastrophe."

Francis R. Steele, an assistant professor of Assyriology in the Department of Oriental Studies at the University of Pennsylvania Graduate School, is among those who refute the local flood view. The presumed evidence of the Ur discovery, he says, has nothing to do with the Biblical Flood.

There are an increasing number of scholars who admit the impossiblity of linking the Ur stratum to the Genesis Flood.

Another argument against the theory is the direction in

which the Ark floated. If it had been a local flood, the Ark would have floated south into the Persian Gulf instead of north. All flood waters flow south in that area, says Dr. Henry Morris, co-author of *The Genesis Flood*.

The depth of the Flood was such that the highest mountains were covered, according to the Bible. "Since water seeks its own level, it would be impossible to confine it to one locality," says physicist George Mulfinger, Jr.

Fossils Indicate Flood

There is more geological evidence in suppport of a global Flood than for any of the other three flood theories.

Such a flood would have to deposit tremendous amounts of sedimentation throughout the world. And it has been scientifically estimated that more than 75 percent of the Earth's surface is sedimentary in nature.

The United States, for example, has immense sedimentary deposits in California, the Colorado plateau and the Midwest plains. India, however, has the deepest known sedimentary deposits—60,000 feet deep!

Geologists have found scores of sedimentary deposits throughout the world where fossilized remains of animals, plants and man-made artifacts—oftentimes from different geographical regions—were dumped into one huge graveyard. Unusual transportation and rapid burial mechanisms, such as a flood, are indicated.

In the northern Rockies, scientists have found well preserved fossilized trilobites and other delicate insect fossils surviving without a sign of disintegration. This suggests that they did not expire slowly, but abruptly, from an unexpected catastrophe, such as a great flood.

The meaning of tiny fossil shells and fish found in rocks seems a mystery, since fish, like other creatures, don't easily become entombed. Immanuel Velikovsky makes this observation about fish in sedimentary rock:

40

When a fish dies, its body floats on the surface or sinks to the bottom and is devoured rather quickly, actually in a matter of hours, by other fish. However, the fossil fish found in sedimentary rock is very often preserved with all its bones intact. Entire shoals of fish over large areas, numbering billions of specimens, are *found in a state of agony*, but with no mark of a scavenger's attack.[2]

Geologist H. Miller, describing the Devonian sedimentary deposit covering much of England, says:

At a period in our history, some terrible catastrophe involved the sudden destruction of fish in an area at least a hundred miles from boundary to boundary. . . .

The same platform in Orkney as at Cromarty is strewed thick with fish remains, which exhibit unequivocally the marks of violent death. The figures are contorted, contracted, curved; the tail in many instances bent around the head; the spines stick out; the fins are spread to the full as in fish that die in convulsions.[3]

The area which Miller describes covers about 20,000 square miles and bears the scars of a destructive force.

Harry S. Ladd of The United States Geological Survey tells of a petrified "fish bed" in Santa Barbara, California, where "more than a billion fish, averaging 6 to 8 inches in length, died on four square miles of bay bottom."[4] The question is: how did they get trapped there, if not by a flood?

Another graveyard believed to be related to flood action is found near Diamondville, Wyoming. This deposit, now a tourist attraction, is furnishing some of the most perfect specimens of fossil fish and plants in the world. Fish from 6 to 8 feet in length and palm leaves from 3 to 4 feet wide have been uncovered.

This confirms the geological theory that the climate was tropical, unlike the blizzard-ridden mountains of Wyoming today. The deposit contained an assortment of other odd remains—alligators, Gar-pike, deep sea bass, sunfish, chubs, herring, pickerel, crustaceans, birds, turtles, mollusca, mammals and varieties of insects.[5]

A Worldwide Mix of Fossils

Such a mixture of organisms from different habitats and climatic regions of the world is characteristic of the most important fossil deposits. Many scientists believe this happened by the "allochthonous process" in which materials are rapidly transported to their final locality and deposited under flood conditions.[6]

This is illustrated by the famous Baltic amber deposits in Eastern Europe, extensively investigated by Dr. Heribert Nilsson, late director of the Swedish Botanical Institute. He says, "The insects discovered there are of fairly modern types [not prehistoric] and their geographical distribution can be ascertained. It is then quite astounding to find that they belong to all regions of the Earth."[7]

As further evidence suggesting the allochthonous process, Dr. Nilsson describes his finds at the lignite beds in Geiseltal, Germany:

Here ... there is a complete mixture of plants and insects from all climatic zones and all recognized regions of the geography of plants or animals.

It is further astonishing that in certain cases the leaves have been deposited and preserved in a fully fresh condition. The chlorophyll is so well preserved that it has been possible to recognize the alpha and beta types. . . .

An extravagant fact, comparable to the preservation of the chlorophyll, was the occurrence of preserved soft parts of the insects: muscles, corium, epidermis, keratin, colour stuffs as melanin and lipochrome, glands and the contents of the intestines. Just as in the case of the chlorophyll, we are dealing with things that are easily destroyed, disintegrating in but a few days or hours. The incrustation must therefore have been very rapid.[8]

Dr. N. D. Newell, paleontologist of the American Museum of Natural History in New York City, recently called the Geiseltal lignite deposits one of the most remarkable examples of preservation of organic tissues in antiseptic swamp waters.

More than six thousand remains of vertebrate animals and a great number of insects, molluscs and plants were found in these deposits. The compressed remains of soft tissues of many of these animals showed details of cellular structure and some of the specimens had undergone but little chemical modification. . . .

Well-preserved bits of hair, feathers and scales probably are among the oldest known examples of essentially unmodified preservation of these structures.

The stomach contents of beetles, amphibia, fishes, birds and mammals provided direct evidence about eating habits.

Bacteria of two kinds were found in the excrement of crocodiles and another was found on the trachea of a beetle. Fungi were identified on leaves.[9]

It is impossible, says Dr. Morris, to account for these vast graveyards in terms of present-day processes and events, "except via the most extreme and unscientific extrapolation."[10] Fossils, he says, give clear evidence of rapid burial, a phenomenon which strongly supports the theory of catastrophism.

"Most of the sedimentary rocks of the Earth's crust, which are the ones containing fossil remains and which therefore provide the chief basis of geologic interpretation of Earth history," Dr. Morris says, "have been laid down as sediments by moving water. (Some have apparently been formed by wind, glaciers or other agencies, but by far the largest part of the sedimentary rocks are aqueous in origin.)"

Still more evidence of a universal flood is apparent in the discovery of artifacts in sedimentary rocks.

An engraved metal bowl, for example, was found in conglomerate rock near Dorchester, Mass., in 1851.

An article in *Scientific American*,[11] indicates that a powerful blast made in rock near Dorchester threw out an immense mass. Some of the pieces weighed several tons. The blast scattered small fragments in all directions.

Among the fragments was a bell-shaped metal pot, 4½ inches high, 6½ inches at the base, 2½ inches at the top and about ⅛ inch thick. It had a zinc color.

On the sides were engraved a bouquet of flowers, beautifully inlaid with pure silver; around the lower part of the pot was a vine inlaid with silver. The carving and inlaying were done exquisitely by a cunning workman.

This agrees perfectly with Biblical chronology. In Genesis 4, metalworking was already highly developed; Tubal-cain was an instructor of every artificer in brass and iron. Gold and silver were also widely used during the same time period.

But the mystery still remains: how did the pot get there if not by flood action?

Another puzzle is the marble block, dug from a quarry about 12 miles northwest of Norristown, Pa., in which were found two raised characters resembling some type of ancient letters. The marble, measuring upwards of 30 cubic feet, was taken from a depth of between 60 and 70 feet and sent to a marble saw mill in Norristown to be cut into slabs. The characters were exposed by the cutting.[12]

Still another mystery is the discovery in England of a gold thread embedded in stone quarried from a depth of eight feet.[13] No one knows how long this remnant of a former age had been embedded.

Doll Found At Great Depth

The late M. A. Kurtz, of Nampa, Idaho, in 1889 discovered a clay female doll at a depth of about 300 feet in a layer of coarse sand as he was boring for an artesian well.

His discovery, called the "Nampa Image," gained the attention of the scientific world.

The 1½ inch doll figurine was found after Kurtz had drilled through about 15 feet of lava rock, 100 feet of quicksand, then six inches of clay, 40 more feet of quicksand, more clay, more quicksand, more clay, then clay balls mixed with sand, then coarse sand.

It has since been called one of the most curious archaeological discoveries of the 19th century and is currently on display at the Idaho Historical Society Museum in Boise.

The significance of the image is this: it represented a man-made object discovered at a depth of about 300 feet. Whoever shaped it had lived on that land 300 feet below the present surface, or it was washed there by the Flood. In either case, it was buried by flood action based on what scientists know of the way sedimentary deposits are laid down.

In Genesis 7 and 8, the deluge buried the pre-Flood civilizations, encasing fossils and artifacts alike in what are now the sedimentary layers of the Earth's crust.

Astronomer's Evidence

Here is another piece of evidence—this time from astronomy—indicating the occurrence of a universal flood.

George F. Dodwell, retired government historical astronomer of south Australia and past director of the Adelaide Observatory, wrote the following letter in the early 1960's to Dr. Arthur J. Brandenberger, presently a professor of photogrammetry at Laval University in Quebec, Canada:

I have been making during the last 26 years an extensive investigation of what we know in astronomy as the secular variation of the obliquity of the ecliptic. From a study of the available ancient observations of the position of the sun at the solstices during the last three thou-

45

sand years, I find a curve which, after allowing for all known changes, shows a typical exponential curve of recovery of the Earth's axis after a sudden change from a former nearly vertical position to an inclination of 26½ degrees, from which it was returned to an equilibrium at the present inclination of 23½ degrees during the interval of the succeeding 3,194 years to A.D. 1850.

The date of the change in the Earth's axis, 2345 B.C., is none other than that of the flood recorded in the Bible, and the resulting conclusion is that the Biblical account of the flood as a universal one, together with its story of Noah's Ark, is historically true.

Traditional Hebrew Bible chronology dates the Flood at about 2448 B.C. while the Greek Septuagint puts it at 3050 B.C.

It seems most reasonable to believe that the Flood took place at least 400 to 900 years before the rise of the great dynasties of the Middle East. The date of the First Dynasty of Egypt based on carbon-14 tests of material from a First Dynasty tomb gives a date range of 2500 to 2100 B.C.

We were unable to verify the contents of Dodwell's letter. In trying to contact Dodwell, we learned he had died in 1963, leaving a surviving son who we have not been able to locate. Most of his papers were willed to the Adelaide Astronomy Society, but officials there say they cannot locate any Flood evidence material among his papers. However, V. J. Bosher, past president of the Society, does remember that Dodwell wrote a 400 page book manuscript on the subject.

We communicated with Dr. Brandenberger to determine his professional opinion of Dodwell's letter. He studied the situation and talked to other astronomers.

"To determine the validity of the Dodwell statement, you need to locate a historical astronomer and I doubt that there is one of those in all of North America," says Dr. Brandenberger. "Today astronomers specialize in branches of astronomy related to space technology and have very little concern for historical astronomy which was Dodwell's specialty.

"Having reviewed the contents of Dodwell's letter among some of my associates at Laval University, it's our conclusion that what Dodwell says could be possible, but we would be very reluctant to accept his assigned dates. In other words we cannot prove or disprove his statements."

We researched the matter further and discovered an article in *Science* magazine (May 15, 1970, vol. 168, pp. 878-880) authored by Rhodes W. Fairbridge of Columbia University. At a meeting of sedimentologists sponsored by the Algerian Institute of Petroleum in January, 1970, Fairbridge asseverated that there had been a polar shift "of sorts" in the past:

> It is assumed that the axis of spin remains more or less constant in terms of celestial mechanics, while it is the earth's lithosphere (earth's crust) that has shifted with respect to the core.

Fossils of Deep Found at Heights

Additional evidence of a universal deluge are fossils found atop Mt. Everest, the highest mountain in the world.

The bones of fish and the shells of sea snails and clams have been found atop Everest and other high peaks. Also, geologists who have climbed Mt. Ararat have discovered shells.

Two lakes in the vicinity of Mt. Ararat provide further signs of a deluge.

Lake Van, in eastern Turkey, is 5,640 feet above sea level and salty. The lake is rich in darekh, a kind of herring.

Lake Urmia, in Iran, is 4,900 feet above sea level. It is 90 miles long and 30 miles wide and shallow—only 20 feet deep at most. Its salt concentration is 23 percent.

Many scientists have said the salt lakes remained after

47

the flood waters had receded. Herring found in Lake Van is a salt water fish prevalent in the North Atlantic today.

Both Lake Van and Lake Urmia are surrounded by high volcanic mountains with no outlet to the sea, so that they remain salty as they were 5,000 years ago.

Dr. Clifford Burdick, a geologist commissioned by the Turkish government to study Mt. Ararat several years ago, found more impressive evidence of a flood.

He found cube shaped salt clusters as large as grapefruit near the 7,000-foot elevation of Mt. Ararat, which he says "indicates that at one time the ocean was thousands of feet higher than it is today.

"As the waters dried up, in some places it left little inland seas of water. And as that dried up, of course, the salt became more concentrated until it precipitated," Dr. Burdick says.

"So it just left these great crystal deposits of salt on the lower slopes of Mt. Ararat."

Pillow lava has been found as high as the 14,000 foot level of Ararat, implying that lava issued from inside the Earth while Ararat was under water. The water rapidly chilled the lava, creating circular formations resembling pillows. This would support Gen. 7:20, which says the flood covered the highest mountains to a depth of 22½ feet.

Dr. Burdick says most of Ararat was formed by volcanic action, and if the glacial ice cap on Ararat did not exist, one would probably find pillow lava all the way to the summit.

Could this pillow lava have been formed during the time of the Flood or because of it?

"Presumably so," Dr. Burdick says. "We don't know of any other time that a mountain that high—17,000 feet— would have been under water. You just have to connect the two. There's no other historical or geological record of the ocean being that high except at that time."

Conglomerate cones found on Ararat, Dr. Burdick says, are further evidence of a universal flood. The conglomerates are various sizes of rocks fused together. They are a mixture of rounded stones, solidified by a cementing

48

medium like calcium carbonate. Lava flow and violent water action are needed to produce them. Finding a conglomerate cone at the 12,000 or 13,000 foot level of Ararat indicates that at one time the area was under water.

Throughout the preceding pages we have seen overwhelming evidence supporting the fact that a universal flood did occur as described in the book of Genesis. But we have not discussed the most critical question relating to this flood. Where did the water come from to flood the earth sufficiently to cover the highest mountains? It's a very critical dilemma—no water, no flood!

Footnotes
Chapter 3

1. Epp, Theodore H., *The God of Creation* (Back to the Bible Broadcast, Lincoln, NE, 1972), pp. 337-338.
2. Velikovsky, Immanuel, *Earth in Upheaval* (Doubleday and Co., New York, 1955), p. 222.
3. Miller H., *The Old Red Sandstone*, p. 221.
4. Ladd, Harry S., "Ecology, Paleontology and Stratigraphy," *Science,* Vol. 129, Jan. 9, 1959, p. 72.
5. "Fishing for Fossils," Vol. 63, *Compressed Air Magazine,* March 1958, p. 24.
6. Whitcomb, John C. Jr. and Morris, Henry M., *The Genesis Flood* (Presbyterian and Reformed Publishing Co., Philadelphia, PA, 1961), pp. 158-159.
7. Heribert-Nilsson, N., *Synthetische Artbildung,* pp. 1195-1196.
8. *Ibid.,* pp. 1195-1196.
9. Newell, N.O., "Adequacy of the Fossil Record," *Journal of Paleontology,* Vol. 33, May 1959, p. 496.
10. Whitcomb and Morris, *op. cit.,* p. 161.
11. *Scientific American,* Vol. 7, No. 38 (June 5, 1852), p. 298.
12. Silman's *American Journal of Science,* 1831, Vol. 29, No. 1., p. 361.
13. *The London Times,* June 22, 1844.

CHAPTER 4

What Are the Necessary Conditions for Producing a Flood?

Any meteorologist will confirm the fact that if every drop of water vapor currently in our atmosphere were suddenly to precipitate throughout the world, the globe would be covered with less than two inches of water.

That's not even enough water to float a rowboat in a local flood, let alone a massive Ark in the worldwide flood described in the Bible. Yet we have shown in an earlier chapter that anthropological accounts from throughout the world support a great deluge. We have also cited numerous scientific evidence that firmly establishes the fact of a universal flood.

Why is there not enough water today to produce a worldwide flood? The explanations are quite simple: (1) rainfall alone did not cause the Flood, even though the Bible says it rained 40 days and 40 nights, and (2) the pre-Flood Earth was vastly different from today.

How was the pre-Flood Earth different? What was its atmosphere? What was the climate like? Were there oceans? What accounts for the fact that today's polar regions once were tropical lands? And the most important question of them all: where did all the water come from?

These and many other questions heighten the mystery surrounding the Flood and its effect on Earth.

"A global rain continuing for forty days, as described in the Bible, would have required a completely different mechanism for its production than is available at the present day," says Dr. Henry Morris, a hydraulics expert who co-authored *Applied Hydraulics in Engineering* and *The Genesis Flood*.[1] "The process of evaporation could

51

not have been effective during the rain, of course, since the atmosphere immediately above the Earth was already at saturation level. The normal hydrologic cycle would, therefore, have been incapable of supplying the tremendous amounts of rain the Bible record describes."

Greenhouse Effect

The concensus among many scholars and scientists is that the antediluvian (pre-Flood) Earth was covered with a water vapor canopy, creating a greenhouse effect on the planet.

Such an effect, due to a permanent cloud cover in the lower atmosphere (the troposphere), would have produced a more favorable environment for life. It would account for animals of the pre-Flood period being much larger than present day counterparts. Butterflies had 20-inch wing spans, and birds with 25-foot wing spans laid eggs 11 inches in diameter.

Also, traditions from many ancient sources suggest that man lived longer and grew taller in a former era. Genesis mentions that man lived as long as nine centuries, a far cry from the current threescore and ten years. As we will see later, an antediluvian canopy would have made longevity possible.

Before moving on, let's look at the Biblical evidence showing that a pre-Flood canopy actually did exist:

And God said, Let there be a firmament [the sky or atmosphere—Webster's Dictionary] in the midst of the waters, and let it divide the waters from the waters. And God made the firmament [atmosphere,] and divided the waters which were under the firmament [oceans, lakes, seas, swamps] *from the waters which were above the firmament* [the water vapor canopy,] and it was so (Genesis 1:6-7).

The greenhouse effect is suggested too in Genesis 2:5,6:

52

And every plant of the field before it was in the earth, and every herb of the field before it grew, for the Lord God *had not* caused it to rain upon the earth, and there was not a man to till the ground. But there went up a mist from the earth, and watered the whole face of the ground.

We can conclude two things from this passage: rain was totally absent in the pre-Flood world and the planet was watered by dew—dependent upon humidity, saturation, temperature, dewpoint and condensation.

"Both of these suggest a lack of planetary wind systems," says Donald Patten, a Seattle, Washington, geographer who has investigated the nature of the Flood from a geographical perspective.

"For instance, dew will form only in the absence of wind. Winds cause rain. But what causes winds? Temperature differentials across the Earth's surface cause wind systems both on a local scale and on a global scale. Today the Earth's atmosphere may be described as one vast wind machine, endeavoring to moderate the recurring temperature differentials across the latitudes and landforms."[2]

Climate Was Unchanging

This would indicate no winds blew in the antediluvian world and that the planet's climate was even throughout.

Further evidence is found in geologic discoveries.

We know, for example, that such desert areas as the Sahara, the Great Australian Desert, the Chilean Atacama and parched regions of the American West once were well-watered, swampy and humid areas.

There is evidence near Cairo of broad-leaf forests that were suddenly entombed and petrified. Petrified forests containing broad-leaf, deciduous trees, coniferous trees, and palms are found in the arid or semi-arid American West. And the trees were large and fast growing—as was other vegetation—also evidence of humid, well-watered regions.

Arctic regions also were tropical.

> The luxuriant growth of broad-leaf hardwood forests in high Arctic latitudes persisted . . . indicating a prolonged continuation of humid, warm temperature, or at least temperate forest climates in polar regions. Evidence for this may be found in both Arctic and Antarctic regions.[3]

Rock fragments from the southernmost known mountain in the world, barely 200 miles from the South Pole, included plant fossils, leaf and stem impressions, coal and fossilized wood—conclusive evidence that the Antarctic climate once was temperate or sub-tropical.[4] Also Adm. Richard Byrd found a petrified forest 100 miles from the South Pole in 1933.[5]

Further evidence of a universally uniform climate is found in the now frigid islands north of Siberia.

An explorer by the name of Baron Toll found a fallen 9-foot fruit tree with ripe fruit and green leaves still on its branches in the frozen ground of the New Siberian Islands. The only tree that grows there today is the one-inch high willow.[6]

Other Planets Suggest Canopies

Patten offers evidence of other planetary canopies and explains suspected features of the Earth's canopy:

> A study of the Earth's atmosphere and its likely ancient greenhouse effect can be better understood by looking briefly at the atmospheres of some of the other nearer planets. Two of the planets have no canopies. They are Mercury and Mars.

> Jupiter and Saturn do not have genuine examples of canopies because a canopy implies that sunlight can penetrate *through* the layer of gas. Venus, is the most interesting planet. In the upper atmosphere of Venus the in-

tense action of solar ultra-violet radiation ... has produced a canopy of carbon suboxide.[7]

The [Earth's] pre-Flood atmosphere was comprised, we suspect, of 3 to 5 times as much water vapor as is today's atmosphere. And, like today, this was concentrated in the lower troposphere.[8]

We suspect that the sea level surface temperature of much of the Earth before the Flood was between 60° and 70°F. [Authors' Note: some scientists place the pre-Flood temperature as high as 90°.] It is proposed that the water vapor canopy was 3,000 to 5,000 feet thick, and ranged between 5,000 and 10,000 feet above sea level.[9]

The pre-Flood atmosphere also is suspected to have contained from 6 to 8 times as much carbon dioxide as the present atmosphere.

Both carbon dioxide and water vapor are efficient at capturing long wave radiation, which happens to be the kind our planet's crust gives off. Hence, in the lower atmosphere, pre-Flood conditions existed in which the *Earth lost very little of its long wave radiation, its heat. Indeed, it retained almost all.* The temperatures of the Earth's surface, it is suspected, were warm on a pole-to-pole basis, and the oceans were similarly warm in high latitudes as well as in low latitudes.

The Earth was lighted by diffused rather than direct light. Short wave (ultraviolet) radiation was filtered out through the upper level ozone layer. The sun's long wave radiation (sun's heat) ... was partly reflected off and what entered was diffused through the water vapor canopy and absorbed by the Earth's surface.[10]

The Earth did not gain a great deal of heat during the daytime, nor did it lose much at night. A temperature equilibrium or near equilibrium was established.[11] The daily temperature range may have been only 2° to 4°F.[12]

Humidity, then, rose to saturation or near saturation level. At night, temperatures dropped only slightly. As dewpoint was reached, a thick layer of nocturnal dew formed. Evaporation during the day would be slow because there was no dry, desiccating wind. Thus the Earth was well watered by abundant condensation and slow evaporation.

A lot of theoretical information has been suggested by geographer Patten about how a pre-Flood canopy would have created a temperature equilibrium. But do we really have any hard evidence from our satellite probes proving a planetary canopy such as the one around Venus actually functions as Patten says the Earth's ancient pre-Flood canopy would have functioned?

Kenneth F. Weaver, assistant editor of *National Geographic,* wrote in an article that the surface temperature of Venus measures about 900° Fahrenheit with a carbon dioxide atmosphere that is a hundred times heavier than the Earth's atmosphere.[13]

"The very density of the atmosphere keeps the intense heat evenly distributed about the planet, with only a few degrees' variation between day and night or between the equator and the poles," says Weaver, based upon information gathered by Mariner 10's flyby of Venus.

"Virtually all experts explain the furnace heat of Venus by the 'greenhouse effect.' Like the glass of a greenhouse, carbon dioxide traps sunlight by preventing its escape as heat. Water vapor does the same. This phenomenon, in fact, makes the average temperature of earth about 90°F higher than it would be if our atmosphere contained no water vapor or carbon dioxide."

Also the article indicated that the Soviet Union's Venera 8, which landed on Venus in 1972, reported that less than 2 percent of the sun's light penetrates the thick canopy cover and reaches the ground. Such light as does get through to the surface is scattered in every direction by diffusion as it travels through the carbon dioxide molecules of the canopy.

This Russian report confirms Patten's idea about the Earth's ancient water vapor canopy deflecting some of the sunlight and diffusing the rest which came through, creating indirect lighting.

God is said to have walked in the Garden of Eden "in the cool of the day" in search of Adam and Eve who were hiding from Him among the trees.

"Cool of the day" seems strange in light of a greenhouse Earth where the daily temperature change was only a few degrees. But Patten explains this:

> With the coming of dusk and the dropping of temperature 2 to 3 degrees, the nearly saturated atmosphere became saturated, as dewpoint was reached. Condensation formed. A chilling layer of dew occurred. This, we suspect, was the "cool of the day." This phrase does not refer to gross temperature decline, but, rather to dewpoint and condensation.[14]

Something above the Earth's surface so affected the incoming solar energy that it maintained a global green house environment. Ozone, carbon dioxide and water vapor are three components of the atmosphere which have this function today, though in significantly lesser measure.

"If one or more of these were a much more abundant constituent of the atmosphere prior to the cataclysm, there would indeed have been a universal 'greenhouse effect,' " says Dr. Morris.[15]

"The most important is water vapor. If there were, in the beginning, a vast thermal blanket of water vapor somewhere above the troposphere, then not only would the climate be affected, but there also would be an adequate source to explain the atmospheric waters necessary for 40 days of rain.

"The favorable climate, aided by the highly effective radiation filter provided by the vapor canopy, would favor abundant plant and animal life, longevity of animal life, and growth of large-sized animal organisms."

Subterranean Waters Added to Flood

Even though we have spent a considerable amount of time discussing the canopy aspect of the Flood, strong evidence in Gen. 7:11 indicates that the waters of the canopy alone could not have inundated the Earth. The Protestant Revised Standard Version of the Bible says, "On that day all the fountains of the great deep burst forth, and the windows of the heavens were opened."

Is there any significance in the fact that Gen. 7:11 says the subterranean waters "burst forth" *before* the "windows of heaven were opened"?

A secondary source of water on the antediluvian Earth existed in vast subterranean heated and pressurized reservoirs either in the primeval crust or in the Earth's mantle. Such a situation exists now, though in lesser quantity.

A number of things could have triggered the stored waters and caused the cataclysm. Dr. Morris suggests a simple explanation: "The pressurized waters below the crust suddenly erupted at a point of weakness. Collapse at one point would cause a chain reaction leading to similar eruptions at many other points around the world."[16]

The resulting atmospheric turbulence, combined with immense amounts of dust blown skyward from volcanos, would begin condensation and precipitation of the canopy, he says. The process would be similar to modern day cloud seeding to cause rain.

Dr. Morris' theory seems valid when we consider the 1883 volcanic eruption of Krakatoa, located between the islands of Java and Sumatra. The following composite report on this eruption was compiled from *The Encyclopedia Britannica* (11th Edition, 1910) and the *Funk & Wagnall's Encyclopedia* (1960):

Until the night of August 26-27, 1883, Krakatoa had an area of about 18 square miles; at that time the most terrific volcanic eruption of modern times destroyed most of the island, so that its present area is only six square miles.

One of the explosions produced the loudest noise ever heard by man; the sound was heard at a distance of 3000 miles. The shock waves produced by the eruption and the accompanying earthquake were felt around the world.

It was·computed that the column of stones, dust and ashes projected from the volcano shot up into the air for a height of 17 miles or more. The finer particles coming into the higher layers of the atmosphere were diffused over most of the earth. Observers world-wide reported brilliant colorations of sunrise and sunset due to the refraction of the sun's rays by these tiny particles.

At Bandong, 150 miles from the center of eruption, the sky was so darkened by the quantity of ashes, that lamps had to be used in the houses at midday. Some of the closest islands received such a thick accumulation of ejected stones and dust as to bury their forests and greatly increase the land mass of the islands. The dust which was shot skyward settled back to the earth over the next three years at a rate of 14 million tons per year.

Tidal waves produced by the eruption attained a height of 50 feet and killed more than 36,000 people along the coasts of Java and Sumatra. Smaller tidal waves were felt at Cape Horn, 7,818 miles from the eruption and in the English Channel, 11,040 miles away.

The dust caused a definite lowering of temperature for two or three years and heavy rains worldwide during the six weeks following the eruption.

Thus we see the possible significance of the order of destruction mentioned in Gen. 7:11. Subterranean upheavals within the oceans, volcanic eruptions and earthquakes and the gushing forth of those waters triggered the opening of the windows of heaven, and the canopy waters poured upon the Earth as torrential rains for 40 days and 40 nights before slacking off to light rain for the next 110 days.

British geologist L. M. Davies, writing about the source of the Flood waters, says, "The question as to where the water came from and where it went to will only trouble those who hold extreme views as to the fixity of oceanic and continental levels. If the sea-beds can rise and the continents sink, there is no difficulty whatever in finding enough water even for a universal flood."[17]

"When we remember that if the whole Earth were perfectly flat the oceans would cover it to a depth of 1½ miles, this statement is obviously true," says Dr. Frederick A. Filby, in his book, *The Flood Reconsidered*. "Either the land sinks or the water level rises . . . or both."[18]

Floods can be caused by the rising of the sea level, and this also seems to be indicated in the Biblical account when reference is made to the Great Abyss or the Great Deep. Ancient people often referred to both the oceans and subterranean waters as the Great Abyss.

"Using the metaphors of ancient languages, the Bible records that the *windows* of heaven were opened and the *fountains* of the Great Deep (Abyss) were broken up. In other words, Noah was conscious of torrential rain and the oncoming of a huge tide, not from swollen rivers, but from the Great Deep, the ocean," says Dr. Filby.

"That the latter (ocean water) was much greater than the former is clearly shown by the fact that the Ark (both in the Biblical and the Babylonian accounts) was carried northwards towards Armenia, whereas a river flood resulting from rain and geyser-type eruptions would have carried it out to the Persian Gulf," explains Dr. Filby.[19]

He contends that many of the great earth movements happened during recent periods and are no doubt directly related to the Biblical Flood catastrophe. "In fact, they increased to a tremendous crescendo," Dr. Filby believes.

A large extension of Southeast Asia has recently sunk beneath the sea until only islands and peninsulas (Borneo, Sumatra, Java, Malaya) remain visible where formerly land was continuous.

So *recent* is the subsidence, the drowned river valleys can still be integrated into a former drainage system, and the distribution of river fish upon the islands still follows the former hydrography.

The whole seaboard of Eastern Asia is drowned in various degrees, and the true margin of the Asiatic block is to be traced along the island festoons which are so marked a feature of that region.

The Sea of Japan is a deeply subsided basin, the East China and Yellow Seas are really shelf, covered by less than one hundred fathoms of water. These inundations have doubtless been caused by subsidence of the continental mass.

There is, of course, much evidence of a very late vertical movement of the Himalaya ... from Tibet into Europe the mountain garland, Hindu Kush, and Caucasus is everywhere the product of uplift during recent times ... volcanic activity built huge cones of andesite or trachyte with basalt ... e.g. *the mountains of Ararat.*[20]

So far, we have discussed three sources for producing enough water for a universal flood: a water vapor canopy, subterranean pressurized reservoirs and the sinking of land masses or the rising of the seabeds. Also we have explained how the subterranean waters and dust released through volcanic eruptions could have started the canopy collapse.

Spark That Set Off the Flood

Dr. Filby states that the greatest source of water came from the oceans and suggests that the spark that collapsed the canopy and caused the subterranean eruptions was a wandering minor planet that flew by at a close distance, causing gravitational havoc.[21]

Geographer Donald Patten has contributed most of the research supporting the fly-by theory. The gravitational pull between these two bodies could have collapsed the canopy, created tidal waves and caused a cataclysm including volcanic eruptions and gigantic sea-bed upheavals.

Patten also suggests that the wandering planet, like some comets, carried with it a vast quantity of frozen gas and ice particles, solids at temperatures like −200 degrees Fahrenheit, and that some of these were captured as electrically charged particles by the Earth's atmosphere.[22]

"Any such 'seeding' of our atmosphere by solid, intensely cold particles as well as meteoric dust would obviously account for the deluge of rain observed by Noah and the vast snowfalls which covered Siberia," says Dr. Filby.[23]

While doing research for this book, we found sufficient evidence to suggest another scientific explanation that could have sparked the Flood. We believe it's plausible that a gigantic meteorite colliding with Earth could have jarred the Earth's crust so tremendously that it set off the universal cataclysmic conditions necessary to have caused the rising of sea-beds, earthquakes, volcanos and the collapse of the water canopy.

The *Encylcopedia Britannica* states that the number of meteorites falling in the centuries before Christ was higher than today. In early times men regarded iron as the metal that fell from the sky.[24]

The meteorite that fell in prehistoric times near Winslow, Arizona, made a hole 4,500 feet across and 600 feet deep. It flung out masses of rock weighing up to 7,000 tons and is estimated to have hurled out altogether 400 million tons of rock. The pressure of the impact exceeded 1,000,000 pounds per square inch, turning silica into new forms known as coesite and stishovite.

The still vaster crater 15 miles across at Ries Kessell in Bavaria also was made in prehistoric times by a meteorite the size of which must have been enormous. One cannot avoid comparison with the great meteorite of 1908 that crashed into the Tunguska valley in Siberia, destroying forests over a radius of twenty miles, and producing earth tremors recorded throughout the world. Although this meteorite probably weighed millions of tons, it must have been small compared with those that long before produced the craters at Winslow and Ries Kessell.

How big would a meteorite have had to be to cause the Flood? And how would it have sparked the Flood?

For answers, let's look at information gathered by satellite photos of Mercury and our moon.

When a huge meteorite, say up to 500 miles in diameter, hits a planet, fast-moving compressive waves move through the planet, followed by slower surface waves. They converge at a point opposite the meteorite impact, shattering land forms and leaving the area in a shambles.

Scientists are quite sure this happened when a huge meteorite collided with Mercury and created the 800 mile wide Caloris basin. The fast-moving compressive waves followed by surface waves moved through the planet shattering the land forms opposite Caloris, creating what scientists call the "weird terrain." Similar shattered land forms exist on the moon opposite great crater basins.[25]

There is little need to speculate on what such an impact would do to the Earth in Biblical times when atmosphere, continents and oceans existed. It would start an indescribable series of events that could easily have sparked the Flood.

Climactic Changes

Regardless of which theory sparked the Flood, the loss of the water vapor canopy altered the Earth's climate and atmosphere.

A significant clue to this is found in Gen. 8:1, ". . . and God made a wind to pass over the earth . . ."

According to geographer Patten, the establishment of the new, post-Flood climate was based on a *new atmospheric organization*. The former low level water vapor in the troposphere had condensed out and vanished. In its stead were irregular, swirling, cyclonic fronts of cloud systems frequenting certain latitudes and not frequenting other latitudes. A permanent and unequal warming of the planet's surface became the new norm. Direct sunlight shone across the latitudes and onto the crust at varying angles, heating surfaces in differing degrees.[26]

The wind was to cause the waters to "return from off the earth."

While the wind would accelerate the evaporation process, evaporation alone could never return to the skies all the water that had fallen in 40 days, to say nothing of subterranean waters.

"The only way in which land could now appear again," says Dr. Morris, "would be for a tremendous orogeny (mountain building process) to take place. Mountains

63

must rise and new basins must form to receive the great overburden of water imposed upon the Earth."[27]

Note Psalm 104:5-9 in reference to the post-Flood:

He established the earth upon its foundations, so that it will not totter forever and ever.* Thou didst cover it with the deep as with a garment; the waters were standing above the mountains. At Thy rebuke they fled; at the sound of Thy thunder they hurried away. The *mountains rose; the valleys sank* down to the place which Thou didst establish for them. Thou didst set a boundary that they may not pass over; that they may not return to cover the earth. (New American Standard Bible).

"The precipitation of the antediluvian vapor canopy instituted a new hydrologic cycle, as well as a new cycle of seasons," Dr. Morris continues.

"A larger proportion of the Earth's surface was now taken up in ocean basins and water surface areas. The pre-antediluvian topography was completely changed, with great mountain chains and deep basins now replacing the formerly gentle and more nearly uniform topography," adds Dr. Morris.[28]

Removal of the canopy also permitted the Earth's atmosphere to be penetrated by much larger amounts of radiation of various types and perhaps also by inter-planetary gas or dust. Increased radiation bathing the Earth's surface is believed to be a cause of the shorter life spans following the Flood—a subject we'll discuss in Chapter 9.

Isostatic adjustments of the rocks and water and other materials near the Earth's surface were also profoundly disturbed and altered.

"And it is obvious that these and other geophysical changes associated with the Flood could not have been completely accomplished and stabilized for centuries," Dr. Morris says.

God's "rainbow" is another result of the post-Flood at-

---

*[This verse may offer further confirmation of Dodwell's contention that the earth's axis shifted during the time of the flood as mentioned in Chapter 3.]

mospheric change. A rainbow is the reflection of sunlight and results when the clouds are most disposed to wet. It comes after a rain and appears when one part of the sky is clear. It first appeared in the sky following the Flood as a sign of God's covenant with Noah that He would never again destory Earth by flood. (Gen. 9:11-17)

In the first four chapters of this book, we have dealt with the mystery of an artifact on Mt. Ararat, the historical accuracy of the Bible, the anthropological evidence for a deluge, the scientific evidence supporting a universal flood, and the environmental conditions present for producing a flood.

But whether or not Noah and his live cargo survived that destructive flood aboard an Ark has not yet been proven.

If the Ark successfully navigated the waters of the Flood, its existence can be established by finding recorded sightings of it, and even ancient artifacts from it—a piece of the "gopherwood" from which it was built, a pot or a tool; some solid evidence that Noah and his family existed and indeed dwelt aboard such a vessel.

Footnotes
Chapter 4

1. Whitcomb, John C. Jr. and Morris, Henry M., *The Genesis Flood* (Presbyterian and Reformed Publishing Co., Nutley, N.J., 1961), p. 121.

2. Patten, Donald, *Symposium on Creation II* (Baker Book House, Grand Rapids, MI, 1970), p. 25.

3. Hooker, Dolph E., *Those Astounding Ice Ages* (Exposition Press, New York, 1948), p. 44.

4. *Ibid.*

5. Patten, Donald, "Cataclysm From Space" filmstrip (American Media, 1971).

6. Hapgood, Charles, "The Mystery of the Frozen Mammoths," *Coronet,* Sept. 1960, p. 74.

7. Patten, *op. cit.,* pp. 13-14.

8. *Ibid.,* p. 14.

9. *Ibid.,* p. 24.

10. *Ibid.,* pp. 14-16.

11. *Ibid.,* p. 26.

12. *Ibid.,* p. 16.

13. Weaver, Kenneth F. "Mariner Unveils Venus and Mercury," *National Geographic,* June 1975, p. 861.

14. Patten, *op. cit.,* p. 27.

15. Morris, Henry M., *Scientific Creationism* (Creation-Life Publishers, San Diego, 1974) pp. 124-125.

16. *Ibid.,* p. 124-125.

17. Lt. Col. L. M. Davies, *J. Trans. Vict. Institute,* 1930.

18. Filby, Frederick A., *The Flood Reconsidered* (Zondervan Publishing Corp., Grand Rapids, MI, 1970), p. 7.

19. *Ibid.,* pp. 7-8.

20. King, Lester C., *The Morphology of the Earth,* pp. 33, 506, 507, 516, 520, and 528. On the southern shores of Lake Van, a salt lake at 5600 feet above sea level near Mt. Ararat, are two clearly defined "raised beaches", one 1600 feet and the other 320 feet above the present level of the lake.

21. Filby, *op. cit.*, pp. 9-11.
22. Patten, Donald W., *The Biblical Flood and The Ice Epoch* (Pacific Meridan Publishing Company, Seattle, WA, 1966) pp. 129-134.
23. Filby, *op. cit.*, p. 11.
24. *Encyclopedia Britannica*, Vol. 15, pp. 275, 276 (1966).
25. Weaver, *op. cit.*, p. 868.
26. Patten, *op. cit.*, p. 28.
27. Whitcomb and Morris, *op. cit.*, pp. 266-267.
28. *Ibid.*, p. 267.

CHAPTER 5

Early Sightings of Noah's Ark

If Noah's Ark did navigate the turbulent waters of the Deluge, and survived the subterranean upheavals, is it still in existence somewhere, waiting to be discovered? Is there any historical evidence for its existence? And has anyone really seen it, or are the alleged sightings merely myths and rumors?

To find evidence of its possible existence, we must know where to look, where the Ark came to rest when the waters receded.

Traditionally the search for the Ark is focused on the "mountains of Ararat" since that's where Genesis says it rested 150 days after the Flood began. The "mountains of Ararat" refers to two volcanic summits—Big (Mount) Ararat and Little Ararat.

Located on the border separating Turkey from the Soviet Union, both history and local legend support the Bible account that the Ark landed on Mt. Ararat.

The Persians call Mt. Ararat Kok-I-Nouh, meaning "mountain of Noah." And there is hardly a place near Mt. Ararat whose name doesn't recall Noah's story.

For example, the town of Nakhitchevan in 100 A.D., was called Apobaterion, meaning "landing place." Its present name means "the first place of lodging." And nearby Temanin translates to mean "place of the eight," which parallels the number of people on the Ark.

Scholars contend that Erivan, a city that seems to have leapt from the pages of the Arabian Nights, is the location where Noah made his first home. Erivan translates to mean "the first appearance."

The village of Seron means "place of dispersion," and

the town of Sharnakh means "village of Noah." Another village called Tabriz or Ta Baris means "the ship."

At the base of Ararat lies the rebuilt part of the ancient town of Ahora, which had been completely destroyed by earthquake in 1840. Arghuri, another name of Ahora, means "the planting of vine." Historians say European wine growing originated from this area where Noah, according to the Bible, "planted a vineyard."

At the nearby Monastery of Echmiadzin, Armenian priests venerate the memory of Noah and his family as the progenitors of the human race. They also have a sacred cross, which they say is made from wood brought from the Ark.

The town of Marand, translated to mean "the mother is here," is the burial place of Noah's wife.

Incidentally, Robert Ripley, the world famous newspaper man and chronicler of the bizarre, joined the search for evidence of Noah's Ark in 1938. He said he had discovered the authentic tomb of Noah.

Writer of the popular "Believe It Or Not" series, with a readership of 80 million in 38 countries, Ripley retained an impeccable reputation over 30 years for never being proven wrong.

According to *The Wall Street Journal* (Feb. 1, 1972) he had many skeptical readers, one of whom has been trying without success to prove Ripley wrong since November 1, 1943. The skeptic, Wayne Harbour, a retired postmaster from Bedford, Iowa, says he investigated at least three *Believe It Or Not* cartoons every day as a hobby. He claims to have written more than 27,000 letters asking for more information and never found an incorrect item.

"In the Lebanon mountains of the Holy Land near the ancient city of Damascus, I found the authentic tomb of Noah," said Ripley in one of his columns. "It is a very sacred and venerable spot in Lebanon as shown by the gifts of clothing, shawls, and household goods brought to the tomb by the faithful." The site today is a tourist attraction.

In Igdir, an old wise man known as Akki Usta is

looked upon as the local historian. He is thought to know all there is to know about the Ark and its secrets.

"The Ark is still on top of the great sorrowful mountain," he says. "Everyone in my village believes this, everyone always has. But to reach it, the only way to reach it, is to be as pure as a young child, free of all evil."

Mt. Ararat has attracted many descriptive names because of local legends. This beautiful, primitive mountain is believed to be "the mountain of evil" by the Kurds; the "mountain of pain" by the Turks; and "the mother of the world" by the Armenians.

Is there really anything mysterious or evil about Mt. Ararat?

According to most local residents of the Ararat area, the mountain is the home of evil spirits and a place of sure destruction for anyone climbing near its summit. But like most superstitions, there are logical explanations for such beliefs.

Permanently Snow Covered

Mt. Ararat's summit is permanently covered by glacial ice and snow. Seldom is the summit visible because it is obscured by misty, fog-like clouds, which create blizzard conditions most of the year. At lower elevations, thunder storms are prevalent.

"Usually, in the morning, the mountain is crystal clear and it's a beautiful sight. But almost every day about ten o'clock, the haze sets in and by three o'clock, there's a storm on Mt. Ararat. At lower elevations, it's a severe thunderstorm while at higher levels it often results in a blizzard," says John Morris, a veteran Ararat climber.[1]

"Because Mt. Ararat is the only glacially covered mountain in that entire region, any evaporation which occurs from the floor or the mountain condenses by mid-afternoon creating the storm conditions," explains Morris.

Mt. Ararat is a volcanic group with two summits—Big Ararat is 16,984 feet, and Little Ararat is 12,806 feet.

Sometimes in the summer, Little Ararat will be without

snow. But the glacial ice cap of Mt. Ararat is more than 200 feet thick, covers about 22 square miles and begins about the 13,000 to 13,500-foot level. Twelve finger glaciers extend from the main glacier, each with its own name.

Cold And Boulders Can Kill

"We spent quite a bit of time camping on the glacier and at night the temperatures would plummet well below zero," says Morris. "The coldest night we ever experienced was on August 3, 1972, when the temperature got down to minus forty and the wind was blowing at about 80 miles per hour. However, during the day time the temperatures usually rise to slightly above freezing."

Often the sound of thunder can be heard on the mountain. But it's not thunder; it's a chain reaction of echoes created as winds up to 150 miles per hour send gigantic boulders crashing down the Ararat slopes. Recent accounts exist of climbers killed by such boulders, which they could hear but not see as they stood in the mists and fogs.

Home To Man's Enemies

There are absolutely no trees on the mountain for shelter, nor wood to build campfires. Most climbers have suffered from the lack of water because melting snow is quickly absorbed through the porous rocks into underground streams. At snowcovered elevations, 100-foot deep crevasses often are not noticed until too late.

The mountain also is home to some of nature's most unfriendly creatures: poisonous snakes, bears and man-attacking wolf dogs.

Adding to the treachery of the mountain are the loose, porous rocks, often causing the climber to slip backward two steps for every three he takes forward. It's impossible to drive a piton in anywhere.

Probably most dangerous are the huge snow and rock

71

avalanches, which climbers set off merely by talking to each other.

Volcanic Action Horrific

Ararat is considered a part of the Taurus mountain chain, which forms the southern part of the Caucasus volcanic chain. It is made of igneous rocks of a porphyroid type, the result of intense volcanic activity that reshaped the northwestern part of Asia several times.

Not only is Mt. Ararat a volcano, it is a strange one. There is no crater on top. Craters are on the sides, particularly on the southwestern slope of Big Ararat.

There is no record of eruption or major earthquake activity during historical times until 1840.

"That year, on July 2," says Ararat explorer Fernand Navarra[2] "a little before sunset, the ground was shaken by undulating waves from the Great Ararat to the east. Fissures appeared on the sides of the mountain, and gas fumes burst out, hurling stones. The ice cap was shattered. Witnesses heard a rumble for an hour within the mountain.

"The village of Ahora disappeared, also the monastery of St. Jacob which had stood for eight centuries. Of the 2,000 and some inhabitants, only a hundred survived—those outside the village itself when the quake struck.

"The Araxes River overflowed and flooded the plain. In the riverbed, craters opened up and water under pressure of gas spurted up in geysers. A few days later, an avalanche of mud from the mountain slopes destroyed the areas spared by the quake. Water from rain, mountain streams, and thawing snow had almost liquefied the earth."

The Ahora Gulch, located on the northeast side of Ararat is a geologic feature of the region. The gulch, blown out of the mountain, has cliffs of 8,000 feet, about twice the depth of the Grand Canyon in Arizona.

The village of Ahora is at the foot of the gulch, probably built on top of the debris that buried the original town in the 1840 earthquake.

Summit Attained By Some

Several explorers have reached the summit of Ararat. The first was Dr. J. J. Friedrich W. Parrot (1791-1841), a respected scholar and the Russian Imperial Councillor of State. He reached the summit Oct. 9, 1829, disproving the belief that the steep, ice-covered peak was impossible to climb.

Major Robert Stuart of England reached the summit in July, 1856. The summit as seen by Stuart and his party is like a scalene triangle. The base, which is on the eastern side, lies nearly due north and south about 100 yards long; the perpendicular is about 300 yards. The area of the triangle is slightly concave. The apex of the triangle is the highest point of the mountain.

"In walking on the summit of Mount Ararat," the Stuart account reads, "one sinks about midway to the knee in the snow, which is so fine and dry that it does not adhere to or wet the boots; but it rises like dust to the wind, blinding the eyes and penetrating the clothes and pockets. The rocks on the sides of the mountain consist chiefly of trachyte porphyry, and the effects of strong volcanic action may be seen wheresoever the natural surface is exposed."[8]

Douglas W. Freshfield (1845-1934), a classical scholar, alpinist and editor of the *Alpine Journal,* came within 1,000 feet of success. His account, published in his *Travels in the Central Caucasus and Bashan* (1869, pp. 155-162), indicates the difficulties explorers have in climbing Ararat. Among them were mountain sickness and horrible headaches because of the altitude and rare air.

Others Died

Tragic deaths have occurred on expeditions up the mountain. The story is told of Christopher Trease who made a solo attempt to climb Ararat in 1965. He carried a moderately heavy pack, but had no ice axe or crampons. He refused an offer of an ice axe at the base of the mountain. The next year an expedition was sent to find his body, but it was never found.

Violet Cummings mentions in her book *Noah's Ark: Fact or Fable?* the accounts of Ararat explorer John Libi. He is said to have witnessed the deaths of two climbers. One, a Belgian in 1967, is said to have fallen more than 300 feet to his death.

Hazards of the Climb

In his book, *The Quest for Noah's Ark,* Dr. John Montgomery gives a vivid description of the difficulties of climbing glacier mountains. Besides winds that blow at more than 100 miles per hour, the ice, especially at the top, is very hard and slippery, steep and dangerous to climb. Breathing is difficult in the thin atmosphere, and it is only by supreme effort and with proper climbing equipment that climbers can hope to succeed.

Lightning strikes, sheer ice cliffs, glacial crevasses, rock that continually breaks off and falls, sometimes at great speeds; cruel blizzards of wind driven snow that comes down in torrents; extreme cold and vicious dogs—all these John Morris encountered on his expedition up the mountain in 1972. He also tells of dodging rocks that flew through the air so fast they spun like a wheel and whistled like shrapnel—each like a buzz saw destroying everything in its path.

Morris in his book, *Adventures on Ararat,* details how his 1972 climbing party was robbed at gunpoint and assaulted by Ararat bandits. Also three of his expedition members were struck by lightning during a severe thunderstorm.

Ancient Scholars Describe Ark

History tells us that in ancient times many men who climbed the mountain in search of the Ark returned to report they had seen it. Accounts from 700 years before the birth of Christ relate the experience of pilgrims climbing

Ararat to scrape tar off the sacred vessel from which to fashion good luck omens.

Berossus, the Babylonian high priest from the temple Bel-Marduk, says that in his time, around 300 B.C., remains of the Ark could still be seen and "some get pitch from the ship by scraping it off, and use it for amulets."[4]

And Hieronymus, an Egyptian historian who authored the ancient history of Phoenicia about 30 B.C., mentions the Ark.

Also about 30 B.C., Nicolaus of Damascus, the biographer of Herod the Great, tells of the Ark landing near the summit and states that relics of the timber were still there.

Nicolaus, who was born about 64 B.C., wrote a vast universal history from earliest times to the death of Herod. He wrote about the Ark in his 96th book as follows:

> There is above the country of Minyas in Armenia a great mountain called Baris, where, as the story goes, many refugees found safety at the time of the flood, and one man, transported upon an ark, grounded upon the summit, and relics of the timber were for long preserved; this might well be the same man of whom Moses, the Jewish legislator wrote.

Josephus, the famous Jewish historian, used Nicolaus' works as one of his sources. He indicated that in his time, too, there were reliable reports that remains of the Ark could be seen. In about 100 A.D. he wrote in his *Antiquities of the Jews*:

> ... the Ark landed on a mountaintop in Armenia. The Armenians call that spot the landing place, for it was there that the Ark came safe to land, and they show the relics of it even today.

> This flood and the Ark are mentioned by all who have written histories of the barbarians, and among these is Berosus the Chaldean. ...

Now I have for witness to what I have said all those that have written antiquities, both among the Greeks and the barbarians. For even Manetho, who wrote the Egyptian History, and Berosus who collected the Chaldean Monuments, and Mochus and Hestiaeus, and besides these Hieronymus the Egyptian, and those who composed the Phoenician History agree to what I say.[5]

St. Theophilus of Antioch in A.D. 180 wrote an account similar to Josephus. He was the sixth bishop of Syrian Antioch, who left his pagan upbringing to become an outstanding apologist for the Christian faith. He wrote:

Moses showed that the flood lasted forty days and forty nights, torrents pouring from heaven, and from the fountains of the deep breaking up, so that the water overtopped every high hill 15 cubits.

And thus the race of all the men that then were was destroyed, and those only who were protected in the Ark were saved; and these, we have already said, were eight.

And of the Ark, the remains are to this day to be seen in the Arabian mountains.[6]

John Chrysostom (345-407 A.D.), patriarch of Constantinople, was considered the greatest preacher of the ancient church. In one of his sermons, he said:

Let us therefore ask them (the unbelieving): Have you heard of the Flood—of that universal destruction? That was not just a threat, was it? Did it not really come to pass—was not this mighty work carried out? Do not the mountains of Armenia testify to it, where the Ark rested? And are not the remains of the Ark preserved there to this very day for our admonition?[7]

Epiphanius of Salamis (315-403 A.D.), a Palestine born monk and Bishop of Constantia, also wrote about the Ark. He was called the "sleuth-hound of heresy," and it was his dream to defend orthodoxy by detecting and refuting heresy in all forms. He wrote:

76

Do you seriously suppose that we were unable to prove our point, when even to this day the remains of Noah's Ark are shown in the country of the Kurds? Why, were one to search diligently, doubtless one would also find at the foot of the mountain the remnants of the altar where Noah, on leaving the Ark, tarried to offer clean and fatly animals as a sacrifice to the Lord God. . . .[8]

Encyclopedists of the early Middle Ages also wrote about the Ark.

"Ararat is a mountain in Armenia," writes Isidore of Seville (560-636 A.D.), the first Christian writer to undertake a compilation of universal knowledge, "where the historians testify that the Ark came to rest after the Flood. So even to this day wood remains of it are to be seen there."[9]

Isidore's encyclopedia entitled *Etymologies* marked its author as one of the most learned men of his age and extended his influence for nearly a thousand years. Today it remains among the most important sources for the history of intellectual culture in the early Middle Ages.

Brother Jehan Haithon, a 13th century Armenian prince who became a Premonstratensian monk in France, is another who wrote about the Ark. He said that in the snow of Mt. Ararat one can see a black spot that is Noah's Ark, which he himself saw in 1254. He writes:

In Armenia there is a very high mountain . . . and its name is Ararat. On that mountain Noah's Ark landed after the Flood . . . at the summit a great black object is always visible, which is said to be the Ark of Noah.[10]

Marco Polo (1234-1324 A.D.), the renowned explorer, says in his book *The Travels*:

And you should know that in this land of Armenia, the Ark of Noah still rests on top of a certain great mountain where the snow stays so long that no one can climb it. The snow never melts—it gets thicker with each snowfall.[11]

77

Vincent Beauvais is another medieval encyclopedist who recorded the survival of Noah's Ark on Ararat. He showed the critical spirit of a modern scholar by carefully screening his authorities. He writes the following about 1256:

> In Armenia there is a noble city called Ani where a thousand churches and a hundred thousand families or households are to be found. . . . Near it is Mount Ararat, where Noah's Ark rests, and at the foot of that mountain is the first city which Noah built, called Laudume.[12]

One of the more fascinating reports comes from the 17th Century Dutch adventurer, Jans Janszoon Struys. In his travel account, he records that while he was in the Ararat region in June of 1670, he was requested to go to a hermitage built on the side of Mt. Ararat to treat a monk with a hernia condition. The monk was so overjoyed with the treatment that he gave Struys one of his most prized possessions, a small wooden cross carved of wood taken from Noah's Ark.

The monk asked him not to keep the wood, but rather to take it to St. Peter's Church in Rome. Realizing the significance of this artifact, Struys requested a written testimony from the monk, which reads as follows:

> I have thought it unreasonable to refuse the request of Jans Janszoon (Struys) who besought me to testify in writing that he was in my cell on the holy Mt. Ararat, subsequent to his climb of some thirty-five miles.

> This man cured me of a serious hernia, and I am therefore greatly in his debt for the conscientious treatment he gave me. In return for his benevolence, I presented to him a cross made of a piece of wood from the true Ark of Noah.

> I myself entered that Ark and with my own hands cut from the wood of one of its compartments the fragment from which that cross is made.

I informed the same Jans Janszoons in considerable detail as to the actual construction of the Ark, and also gave him a piece of stone which I personally chipped from the rock on which the Ark rests. All this I testify to be true—as true as I am in fact alive here in my sacred hermitage.

Dated the 22nd of July, 1670, on Mt. Ararat—Domingo Alessandro of Rome.[13]

Sir John Chardin (1643-1713 A.D.), a Frenchman who was knighted by English monarch Charles II in 1681, reflects some skepticism, however, in stories about the Ark:

Twelve leagues to the east of Erivan one sees the famous mountain where almost everyone agrees that Noah's Ark landed—though no one offers solid proof of it.

The Armenian traditions relate that the Ark is still upon the summit of this Mount Massis (Ararat). They add that no one has ever been able to climb to the place where it came to rest. This they firmly believe on the basis of a miracle said to have happened to a monk of Echmiadzin named Jacob, who later became Bishop of Nisibis. They relate that this monk was determined to climb to the summit or die in the attempt.

He got halfway up, but he could never go higher, for after climbing all day he was miraculously carried back—while asleep at night—to the same spot from which he had set out in the morning. This went on for some time in this fashion, when finally God gave ear to the monk's vows and determined to satisfy his desires in part. Consequently, by an angel he sent to him a piece of the Ark, exhorting him through this messenger not to fatigue himself to no purpose in climbing the mountain, for God had forbidden mankind to have access to its summit.

That's the story, and I have two things to say concerning it. First, it is at variance with the ancient writers, such as Josephus, Berossus, and Nicolaus of Damascus, who assure us that in their time the remains of the Ark were still to be seen, and that powder made from the bitumen with which it had been pitched was taken as a preservative of health.

Secondly, instead of its being a miracle that no one could ever reach the top of this mountain, I should rather deem it a great miracle if anyone *did* reach its summit! For the mountain is without any habitation, and from the halfway point to the peak it is perpetually covered with snow which never melts, so that at all seasons it has the appearance of a gigantic mass of snow.[14]

Early Historians Discussed Ark

There is an impressive collection of Middle East reports dealing with the Ark by historians from the Mesopotamia and Palestinian areas. Major accounts were written by those who spent their lives in and around the cradle of civilization—men who grew up with the historical accounts of the Flood.

Odoric, a Bohemian of Friuli near Pordenone in northern Italy, was a medieval Franciscan monk who is remembered mainly for a narrative of his wanderings in the Far East. He wrote that he had wanted to climb Ararat in search of the Ark but was told that no one could ascend the mountain because it would displease God.

"The Ark's presence on Ararat was a matter of such common opinion in the medieval period that merchants could use the expression 'under Noah's Ark' as a synonym for Ararat without even mentioning the latter," says Dr. Montgomery, professor of law and theology at the International School of Law in Washington, D.C. This fact, he says, shows up in an ancient list of toll stations in the Armenian country.[15]

A legend that climbing the mountain would displease God possibly originates from the grave misfortunes of those who tried to find the Ark. Because of such misfortunes, pilgrimages came to an end. And the mountain itself has become a part of this ancient mystery.

Even today, a main hindrance to expeditions is the Kurds of the area. Out of fear and superstition, Kurdish guides are usually unreliable.

In 1876, climber James Bryce's guides left him at the ice cap, and he had to continue alone. In 1969, Eryl Cummings had a similar experience. He had been thrown from a horse against a rock, and was in pain. He needed the help of his porters, but when they reached the 13,000 foot elevation, they refused to go further. He gave them more money, but after they went another 500 feet, they refused to continue.

Since the Kurds are the local residents of the villages around Ararat, most expeditions must depend on them to act as guides and porters. More often than not, they refuse to climb beyond the lower snow levels, or desert the expedition during the cover of night, leaving the foreigners to fend for themselves—to survive by good fortune or to perish, as many have during the past 200 years.

Footnotes
Chapter 5

1. Statements made by John Morris during a February 1976 interview.

2. Navarra, Fernand, *Noah's Ark: I Touched It* (Logos International, Plainfield, N.J., 1974), p. 121.

3. Stuart, Robert, *Proceedings of the Royal Geographical Society,* (1877), pp. 77-92.

4. Text in *Eusebi chronicorum libri duo,* ed. Alfred Schoene, Vol. I (Berlin, 1875) col. 20-24. Translated by A. M. Harmon in A.T. Clay, *A Hebrew Deluge Story in Cuneiform* (New Haven, CT, 1922), pp. 82-83.

5. Josephus, Flavius, *Antiquities of the Jews.*

6. Book three of *Ad Autolycum* by Theophilus. Passage from Marcus Dods' translation in the *Ante-Nicene Fathers,* (1885, II, 117).

7. From a sermon given by John Chrysostom, Latin translation from the Greek text by Migne, *Patrologiae cursus completus . . . series graeca, LVI,* cols. 287-88.

8. Taken from *Panarion,* I.i 18 (the chapter refuting the beliefs of the Nazarenes, whom Epiphanius classes as the fifth variety of Judaizing heresy). Translation from F. Oehler's *Corpus haereseologicum.* II/1 (Berlin, 1859), 94-95.

9. Isidore's *Etymologies.* Translated from Vol. II of W. M. Lindsay's critical edition of the Latin text of Isidore's *Etymologies* (1911); the passage, in the section "On Mountains," is designated XIV, 8.5, and a collateral reference to the landing of the Ark in the mountains of Armenia occurs at XIV, 3.35.

10. Translation from Backer's French text: *L'Extreme Orient au moyen age* (1877), p. 145. From Haithon's account "Marvels of the Thirteen Kingdoms of Asia."

11. Marco Polo, *The Travels,* ed. and trans. Ronald Latham (The Folio Society, London, 1968), p. 34.

12. *Speculum quadruplex* by Vincent of Beauvais (1256-

1259). Translation from p. 1266 of the 1624 Douai ed. of the *Speculum*.

13. Translated from Struys' account of his third voyage, Chapter 18 in *Les Voyages . . . en Moscovie, en Tartarie, en Perse, aux Indes, & en plusieurs autres Pays étrangers* (1684), II, pp. 146-62.

14. Translated from Sir John Chardin's *Voyages . . . en Perse, et autre lieux de l'Orient* (II, pp. 235-37) French edition at Amsterdam in 1711.

15. Montgomery, John Warwick, *The Quest for Noah's Ark* (Bethany Fellowship, Inc., Minneapolis, MN, 1972) p. 87.

CHAPTER 6

Expeditions and Sightings of the 1800's

Early history reveals many sightings of Noah's Ark, but not until recently have major expeditions scaled the dangerous slopes of Ararat to bring back what is believed to be evidence of the Ark's existence.

One reason for the early lack of expeditions was apparently the treachery of Ararat's glacier covered summit. Also, for long periods of time, the summers were not warm enough to melt the glacier sufficiently to expose the ice-embedded Ark or to permit climbers to reach the summit safely. A third reason is that Europeans were preoccupied with other interests and discoveries during the latter part of the Middle Ages.

But in 1829, Ararat's summit was reached.

The first historically recorded ascent was made by a Russian-born, German physician named Dr. J. J. Friedrich W. Parrot. Dr. Parrot, who was a professor at the University of Dorpat in Russia, was the first known modern explorer to:

> 1. Visit the Armenian monastery at Echmiadzin, where he saw an artifact said to have been made from a piece of wood from Noah's Ark.
>
> 2. Visit St. Jacob's Monastery at Ahora where supposedly ancient Noahic relics and a manuscript were kept.
>
> 3. Conquer the mountain by reaching its summit.

Parrot's expedition was made in 1829 when little was known about mountain climbing. He had heard claims that at the monastery at Echmiadzin there was a relic said to be made from the sacred wood of Noah's vessel. He describes what he saw:

... The real treasures of this monastery ... are the holy relics which are preserved in the cathedral, deposited each in its own chest. They are never exhibited but on some particular occasions.

The objects respecting which I obtained any specific information I shall mention somewhat in detail. The hand of St. James, enclosed in a hand of the natural shape, with an arm, of silver gilt: the thumb and fore-finger are bent towards each other, and between them hangs a fragment of the ark of Noah, by a little chain: it is a small, dark-coloured, quadrangular piece of wood, in good preservation, and carved upon one surface.[1]

After seeing the relic, Dr. Parrot journeyed up Ararat to the 7,000-foot level. There he visited the St. Jacob Monastery at Ahora, which contained priceless remains of Noah's great voyage. He continued his climb and reached the summit.

The following are excerpts from his account:

We were obliged to leave one of the peasants behind at the place where we spent the night, as he complained of illness; two others tired in ascending the glacier, stopped at first only to rest, but afterwards went back to the same station. The rest of us, without allowing ourselves to be detained an instant by these accidents, pushed on unremittingly to our object, rather excited than discouraged by the difficulties in our way . . . .

We passed without stopping over a couple of hills, there we felt the mountain wind; I pressed forward round a projecting mound of snow, and behold! Before my eyes, now intoxicated with joy, lay the extreme cone, the highest pinnacle of Ararat. Still, a last effort was required of us to ascend a tract of ice by means of steps, and that accomplished, about a quarter past three on the ninth October, 1829, we stood on the top of Ararat.

Formed of eternal ice, without rock or stone to interrupt its continuity, it was the austere, silvery head of Old Ararat. Towards the east, this summit extended more uniformly than elsewhere, and in this direction it was connected by means of a flattish depression, covered in like manner with perpetual ice, with a second and somewhat lower summit ... only 397 yards, or less than a quarter of a mile (away).

The gentle depression between the two eminences presents a plain of snow moderately inclined towards the south, over which it would be easy to go from the one to the other, and which may be supposed to be the very spot on which Noah's Ark rested, if the summit itself be assumed as the scene of that event, for there is no want of the requisite space, inasmuch as the Ark, according to Genesis 6:15, three hundred ells long and fifty wide, would not have occupied a tenth part of the surface of this depression.[2]

Some have wondered how a boat could rest on a mountain peak without tumbling down as few, if any, of the mountains in the world have a level plateau at their summits on which a boat could land safely. But the plateau at the top of Ararat would make such a grounding possible.

Dr. Parrot's account continues:

Ker Porter, however, makes on this subject a subtle comment favourable to the opinion that the resting-place of the Ark was not on the summit of the mountain, but on some lower part of it; because in Genesis 8:5, it is said, "On the first day of the tenth month the tops of the mountains came forth;" but in 6:16, it is stated that the window of the Ark was above; consequently, Noah could have seen only what was higher than the ship, which was therefore lower down than the tops of the mountains.[3]

Earthquake Described

St. Jacob's Monastery at Ahora (also called Arghuri, Ahuri or Aghurri), where Parrot saw Ark relics, was destroyed by an earthquake 11 years later. The monastery and village were covered with debris during the destruction of June, 1840.

James Bryce wrote in 1877 about the 1840 quake:

> There formerly stood a pleasant little Armenian village of some two hundred houses, named Arghuri, or Aghurri. ... Not far above the village ... stood the little monastery of St. Jacob, eight centuries old. Towards sunset in the evening of the 20th of June, 1840, the sudden shock of an earthquake, accompanied by a subterranean roar, and followed by a terrific blast of wind, threw down the houses of Arghuri, and at the same moment detached enormous masses of rock with their superjacent ice from the cliffs that surround the chasm.

> A shower of falling rocks overwhelmed in an instant the village, the monastery, and a Kurdish encampment on the pastures above. Not a soul survived to tell the tale. ...

> ... The little monastery, where Parrot lived so happily among the few old monks who had retired to this hallowed spot from the troubles of the world, is gone for ever; no Christian bell is heard, no Christian service said, upon the Mountain of the Ark.[4]

Others Reach Summit

After Parrot's adventures on Ararat, other climbers came exploring, seeking ... hoping to bring back physical evidence proving that the Ark still existed on Mt. Ararat.

In 1835, Karl Behrens climbed the mountain, and said he saw the cross planted on the summit by Parrot. He did not see the Ark. His ascent was attested by the Imperial Russian Geographical Society.

Russian geologist, Hermann von Abich,[5] after three unsuccessful tries, finally reached the eastern summit on July 29, 1845. He was only 30 feet lower and a six minute walk from the western summit conquered by Parrot when he retreated due to threatening weather. The eastern summit today is named after Abich.

H. Danby Seymour made the ascent in 1846. Since his expedition could get no porters, one of the Armenians in his company served as a guide. But the guide refused to come until Seymour gave him his own boots and wore some Persian slippers.

"We had to carry all we wanted for our ascent ourselves," Seymour wrote.[6] "I remember I had chickens fastened around my waist."

The climbers could not stay on the summit long since the clouds began to gather about them.

In 1850 Col. Khodzko[7] of the Russian Army reached the peak. His expedition was well organized and conducted in full cooperation with the local authorities. Sixty persons participated in the expedition with the intent to establish a long-term operation on the peak during which the team could make a thorough, scientific search for the Ark.

The expedition was plagued by furious wind, lightning and thunder, fog, thick snow flurries, hail and ice. But the climbers overcame these obstacles and reached the peak that Parrot had attained years before. Because of severe weather conditions on Ararat, the long-term operation fizzled.

Major Robert Stuart, an Englishman, led an expedition to the summit in 1856. They experienced similar difficulties. The significance of his climb, gleaned from a report in his private journal, published in 1887 in the *Proceedings of the Royal Geographical Society,* (pp 77-92) is his reference to the local belief in the Ark's survival on the mountain.

The popular belief throughout Central Asia, he said, was that the Ark had come to rest on Aghri Dagh or Mt. Ararat. Here is an excerpt from his report:

The Kurdish tribes who dwell on the slopes and at the base of Aghri Dagh, and whose forefathers have been there since the earliest dawn of history, the native Christians of Georgia and Armenia—all indeed who preserve the traditions of the land—are familiar with the story of the Deluge. Their account of that great event varies but slightly from that which has been transmitted to us by Moses, and they hold it as part of their faith that Noah's Ark rested on Aghri Dagh, that the hull still remains on the summit, deeply buried out of sight . . .

Stuart's expedition, like the many others, had to make the final assault on the summit without the Kurds, who refused to continue for fear of God's wrath and local superstitions.

Scientists Try To Destroy Ark

What is thought to be the earliest known modern day discovery of Noah's Ark, occurring somewhere between 1850 and 1880, is indicated in the story told by Haji Yearam, an Armenian who lived out his final days in America. The story is recounted by Harold H. Williams, who in 1952 was pastor of the Seventh Day Adventist Church in Logansport, Indiana. Here are excerpts:

Haji Yearam's parents and family lived at the foot of Greater Mount Ararat in Armenia. According to their traditions, they were descended directly from those who had come out of the Ark, but who had never migrated from that country. Haji's forebears had always remained near the mount where the Ark came to rest in a little valley surrounded by some small peaks. . . .

For several hundreds of years after the flood, his forebears had made yearly pilgrimages up to the Ark to make sacrifices and to worship there. They had a good trail and steps to the steep places. Finally the enemies of God undertook to go to Ararat and destroy the Ark, but as they neared the location there came a terrible storm that washed away the trail, and lightning blasted the rocks. From that time on, even the pilgrimages ceased, because they feared to betray the way to the ungodly, and they feared God's wrath.

When Haji was a large boy, but not yet a man fully grown, there came to his home some strangers. There

89

were three vile men who did not believe in the Bible and did not believe in the existence of a personal God. They were scientists. They were on this expedition specifically to prove the legend of Noah's Ark to be a fraud and a fake.

They hired the father of young Haji Yearam as their official guide. They hired the boy to assist his father as guide.

It was an unusually hot summer, so the snow and glaciers had melted more than usual. After extreme hardship and peril the party came to the little valley way up on Greater Ararat, not on the very top but a little way down from the top. This little valley is surrounded by a number of small peaks. There the Ark came to rest in a little lake, and the peaks protected it from the tidal waves that rushed back and forth as the flood subsided. On one side of the valley the water from the melting snows and glacier spills over in a little river that runs down the mountain. As they reached this spot, there they found the prow of a mighty ship protruding out of the ice.

Scientists Enter Ark

They went inside the Ark and did considerable exploring. The whole structure was covered with a varnish or lacquer that was very thick and strong, both outside and inside the ship. The ship was built more like a great and mighty house on the hull of a ship, but without any windows. There was a great doorway of immense size, but the door was missing.

The scientists were appalled and dumbfounded and went into a rage at finding what they had hoped to prove non-existent. They were so angry and mad that they said they would destroy the ship, but the wood was more like stone than any wood we have now. They did not have the tools or means to wreck so mighty a ship and had to give up. They did tear out some timbers and tried to burn the wood, but it was so hard it was almost impossible to burn it.

They held a council, and then took a solemn and fearful death oath. Any man present who would ever breathe a word about what they had found would be tortured and murdered.

They told their guide and his son that they would keep tabs on them and that if they ever told anyone and they found it out they would surely be tortured and murdered. For fear of their lives, Haji and his father had never told what they found except to their best trusted and closest relatives.[8]

Deathbed Confession

Haji's story was confirmed by an elderly scientist on his deathbed in London, Williams said. His report continues:

One evening (I am pretty sure it was in 1918) I sat reading the daily paper in our apartment in Brockton. Suddenly I saw in a very small print a short story of a dying man's confession. It was a news item one column wide and, as I remembered it, not more than two inches deep. It stated that an elderly scientist on his deathbed in London was afraid to die before making a terrible confession. It gave briefly the very date and facts that Haji Yearam had related to us in his story.

Haji Yearam had died in my parents' home in Oakland, California, about the same time that the old scientist had died in London. We had never for a moment doubted Haji's story, but when this scientist on his deathbed on the other side of the world confessed the same story in every detail, we knew positively that the story was true in every detail.[9]

Evidence Brought Back

Sir James Bryce, a highly regarded British statesman, jurist and author, made a dramatic and first-time ever solo ascent of the mountain in 1876. He returned with a piece of evidence that should have shocked the scientific world into action.

Braving the hostile environment of Ararat, Bryce uncovered and brought back to London a four-foot long, five inch thick piece of partially petrified, hand-tooled timber.

He found the wood at about 13,000 feet—where no trees had ever grown.

Although newspaper headlines hailed the event, scientists scoffed at it.

The following includes excerpts of his expedition, taken from his published accounts:[10]

My friend and I started from Aralykh, a Russian military station on the right bank of Araxes . . . at 8 a.m. on the morning of Monday, September 11, 1876, with an escort of five mounted Cossacks, who were supposed to be needed as protection against robbers. . . .

Passing a small Kurdish encampment, we reached, at 2 p.m., the highest Cossack military post—Sardarbulach. . . . The height is nearly 8,000 feet above the sea. . . . We were anxious to push on. Horses, however, could not be taken further; the Cossacks refused to carry even the trifling load of provisions and wrappings required for sleeping in the open air, and by the time that Kurds had been collected and a bargain made with them it was past four o'clock, too late to get far up before nightfall.

Night Trip

Reluctantly, therefore, we halted at Sardarbulach and got some sleep from nine o'clock till midnight. At 1 a.m., the crescent moon having risen high enough to give a little light, we set off with four Kurds carrying our baggage, and no less than seven Cossacks . . . .

The progress of this caravan over the rocky ground, traversed by rough volcanic ridges, which we had to cross in our north-western course towards the cone from Sardarbulach, was very slow, not only owing to the darkness, but also because the Cossacks insisted on sitting down to rest whenever the track became steeper than usual. At 7 a.m. the whole party stopped at a height of about 12,000 feet, just where the first snow appeared, laid down the sleeping apparatus, and made it quite clear to us they would go no further.

At eight o'clock I buckled on my canvas gaiters, thrust some crusts of bread, a lemon, a small flask of cold tea, four hard-boiled eggs, and a few meat lozenges into my pocket, bade good-bye to my friend, and set off. Rather to our surprise, the two Cossacks and one of the Kurds came with me, whether persuaded by a pantomime of encouraging signs, or simply curious to see what would happen.

The ice-axe had hugely amused the Cossacks all through. Climbing the ridge to the left, and keeping along its top for a little way, I then struck across the semicircular head of a wide glen, in the middle of which lay a snowbed, over a long steep slope of loose broken stones and sand. However, on the other side, I got upon solid rock, where the walking was better.

Wood Sighted

The summit of Little Ararat, which had for the last two hours kept provokingly at the same apparent height above me, began to sink, and before ten o'clock I could look down upon its small flat top, studded with lumps of rock, but bearing no trace of a crater.

Mounting steadily along the same ridge, I saw at a height of over 13,000 feet, lying on the loose blocks, *a piece of wood* about four feet long and five inches thick, evidently cut by some tool, and so far above the limit of trees that it could by no possibility be a natural fragment of one.

Darting on it with a glee that astonished the Cossack and the Kurd, I held it up to them and made them look at it, and repeated several times the word "Noah". The Cossack grinned, but he was such a cheery, genial fellow that I think he would have grinned whatever I had said. . . . Whether it was really gopherwood, of which material the Ark was built, I will not undertake to say, but I am willing to submit to the inspection of the curious. . . .

And if there be any remains of the Ark on Ararat at all—a point as to which the natives are perfectly clear—here, rather than the top is the place where one might expect to find them, since in the course of ages they would get carried down by the onward movement of the snow-beds along the declivities. This wood therefore suits all the requirements of the case.

Shortly after the find, Bryce was deserted by the two Cossacks and the Kurd and had to continue his ascent alone.

Papers Ridicule

Seven years later, in August 1883, the Turkish government announced its discovery of Noah's Ark. It was the first official comment by the Turkish authorities of the Ark's existence. The story appeared in leading American newspapers across the country. Here we quote from the August 10, 1883 issue of the *Chicago Tribune*:

A paper at Constantinople announces the discovery of Noah's Ark. It appears that some Turkish commissioners appointed to investigate the question of avalanches on Mt. Ararat suddenly came upon a gigantic structure of very dark wood protruding from a glacier. They made inquiries of the inhabitants.

They had seen it for six years, but had been afraid to approach it because a spirit of fierce aspect had been seen looking out the upper window. The Turkish commissioners, however, are brave men, not deterred by such trifles, and they determined to reach it. Situated as it was among the fastness of one of the glens of Mt. Ararat, it was a work of enormous difficulty, and it was only after incredible hardship that they succeeded.

The Ark was in a good state of preservation, although the angles—observe, not the bow or stern—had been a good deal broken in its descent. They recognized it at once.

There was an Englishman among them who had presumably read his Bible, and he saw that it was made of the ancient gopherwood of Scripture, which, as everyone knows, grows only on the plains of the Euphrates.

Effecting an entrance into the structure, which was painted brown, they found that the admiralty requirements for the conveyance of horses had been carried out, and the interior was divided into partitions fifteen feet high. Into three of these only could they get, the others being full of ice, and how far the Ark, extended into the glacier they could not tell. If, however, on being uncovered, it turns out to be 300 cubits long, it will go hard with disbelievers.

The Turkish government, irked at discouraging treatment by the world's newspapers and scientific leaders, did not follow up the discovery with another expedition.

Nouri—Did He or Didn't He?

Four years later, however, the magnetic and astonishing Prince John Joseph Nouri announced that he would mount an expedition in an attempt to locate the Ark.

Nouri, the archdeacon of Babylon and of the Malabar, India Christian Nestorian Church, was only 22 when he began his ascent in 1887. On April 25th of that year, he saw Noah's Ark, the story goes.

Prince Nouri reported that he "found the Ark wedged in the rocks and half filled with snow and ice . . . that it was made of dark beams of very thick wood."[11] His account gave support to the 1883 Turkish account.

He hoped to return to Ararat with a major expedition to take the vessel off the mountain before it froze over again, or before it fell deeper into a greater crevasse, disappearing perhaps for centuries. The prince wanted to take the Ark to the Chicago Exhibition, the World's Fair of 1893, but he was not able to obtain financial support.

The prince's secret—his route to the Ark on Mt. Ararat—was lost forever when he died unexpectedly from pneumonia.

By 1945, Nouri's name had become a legend, though many high-ranking individuals in the religio-scientific world claimed he never existed.

Archaeologist Dr. J. O. Kinnaman came to Nouri's defense:

> "Regarding the famous Dr. Nouri, one of the greatest scholars and world-wide travellers the last quarter of the 1880s ever saw," he wrote on August 16, 1946, "allow me to state that at the World Parliament of Religions, World's Fair, Chicago, Ill., in 1893, I had the honor and pleasure of meeting Dr. Nouri personally, and conversing with him several times.

> "There is no mistake that he actually lived, walked and talked upon the Earth, for I am sure I was not talking with a ghost. Some maintain that no such man ever lived. Well, if he did not, then there are hundreds of thousands of liars in India. I spent three years in India at the beginning of the century, and heard them comment on his life and works."[12]

Nouri's existence also was confirmed by Dr. John Henry Barrows, president of the World Parliament of Religions, who had personally invited the prince to attend the convention.[13]

One of the significant facts of Nouri's discovery is that the measurements of the Ark coincided exactly with the account given in the sixth chapter of Genesis.[14]

Flamboyant Prince Nouri closed the chapter on expeditions and sightings of the 19th century. It was a century of big gains in the quest for Noah's Ark. The conquest of Mt. Ararat was achieved. Wood believed to be from the Ark was recovered from Ararat's snow covered slopes.

The first official recognition by any government concerning the discovery of Noah's Ark was made.

The discovery and actual attempt by some scientists to destroy the Ark made the 19th century an intriguing era for the Ark searchers. But the 20th century had even greater gains in store for the ark-eologists, due to renewed interest and the uses of modern scientific technology.

Footnotes
Chapter 6

1. Parrot, J. J. Friedrich W., *Journey to Ararat* (1845) pp. 101-102.

2. *Ibid.*, pp. 176 ff of the English edition.

3. *Ibid.*, pp. 176 ff.

4. Bryce, Sir James, *Transcaucasia and Ararat* (1877) pp. 239-241.

5. von Abich, Hermann, Bulletin *de la Société de Geographié*, (1851), pp. 521-523.

6. Freshfield, Douglas W., "Early Ascents of Ararat," *Alpine Journal,* (1877) vol. VIII, pp. 214-216.

7. Longuinoff, D., "Ascension de l' Ararat," Bulletin *de la Société de Geographié*, (1851) Vol. I, pp. 52-65.

8. Cummings, Violet M., *Noah's Ark: Fable or Fact?* (Family Library, New York, 1975), pp. 113-115.

9. *Ibid.*, pp. 115-116.

10. Bryce, Sir James, "The Ascent of Ararat," *Alpine Journal,* VIII, 1877; *Transcaucasia and Ararat,* 1877; and "On Armenia and Mount Ararat," *Proceedings of the Royal Geographical Society,* XXII, 1878.

11. Coan, Frederick G., *Yesterdays in Persia and Kurdistan* (Saunders Studio Press, Claremont, CA, 1939), p. 163.

12. Cummings, Violet M., *Noah's Ark: Fact or Fable?* (Creation-Science Research Center, San Diego, CA, 1972), p. 120.

13. *Ibid.*

14. Coan, *op. cit.,* p. 105.

CHAPTER 7

Ark Sightings Furnish Detailed Descriptions

The two most spectacular sightings of the Ark since the 1883 Turkish discovery were made by George Hagopian in 1902 and Russian aviator Vladimir Roskovitsky in 1916. These two sightings have supplied us with the most detailed description of the Ark as it exists on Mt. Ararat in the 20th century.

Hagopian, an 80-year-old Armenian, was taken up the slopes of Mt. Ararat by his uncle to see Noah's Ark in 1902. He was 10 years old then and was a shepherd boy who looked after sheep on the mountain slopes.

Here are excerpts from his story recorded in Easton, Maryland, in 1970, during a taped interview with Ark researchers Elfred Lee and Eryl Cummings:

My grandfather was the minister of the big Armenian Orthodox Church in Van (near Lake Van), and he always told me stories about the holy ship on the holy mountain.

And then one day my uncle said, "Georgie, I'm going to take you to see the holy Ark." We packed supplies on his donkey, and together we started our trek toward Mt. Ararat.

My feet were getting sore, and the donkey kept wanting to go in the wrong direction, but we continued climbing until we got about halfway up. Then Uncle took both supplies and me on his back, and we climbed and climbed.

It took us almost eight days from the time we left Van to the moment we got to the place on the holy mountain where both my grandfather and my uncle had said the holy ship had come to rest.

I guess my uncle took me there that year because it was a year without much snow—a "smooth year" we called it. There's one of those about every twenty years.

Boy Climbs On Top Of Ark

And then we got to the ark. It was getting dark and misty around us. My uncle dropped his pack, and together we began to haul stones to the side of the ship. Within a short time we had stacked a high pile of rocks against the side of the ship.

"Georgie, come here" he said, grabbing me by the arm. "You are going on top of the holy ark." He lifted me up and put me on his shoulders, and together we climbed the pile of rocks. When he had reached the top, his hands grabbed my ankles and he began to push me up.

"Reach for the top, Georgie," he yelled. "Grab the edge and pull yourself up!"

I stood up straight and looked all over the ship. It was long. The height was about forty feet.

"Look inside the ark," my uncle called up to me. "Look for the holes. Look for the big one. Look inside and tell me what you see."

I shivered from the cold and from fear and glanced around me. Yes, there was the hole, big and gaping. I peeked into the blackness of the hole, but saw nothing. Then I knelt down and kissed the holy ark.

When we were there, the top of the ark was covered with a very thin coat of fresh fallen snow. But when I brushed some of it away I could see a green moss growing right on top. When I pulled a piece off ... it was made of wood. The grain was right there. This green moss made the ark feel soft and moldy.

On the roof, besides one large hole, I remember small holes running all the way from the front to the back. I don't know exactly how many, but there must have been at least fifty of them running down the middle with small intervals in between. My uncle told me these holes were for air.

That roof was flat with the exception of that narrow raised section running all the way from the bow to the stern with all those holes in it.

I remember, my uncle took his gun and shot into the side of the ark, but the bullet wouldn't penetrate. Uncle then pulled his long hunting knife from his belt, and with the heavy handle he chipped a piece from the side of the ark. Then we went down the mountainside and returned to Van.

Ark Visited Second Time

Hagopian saw the ark two years later while on a pilgrimage for "Holy" flowers. He adds more descriptive details concerning the Ark's appearance:

I saw the ark a second time. I think it was in 1904. We were on the mountain looking for holy flowers, and I went back to the ark and it still looked the same. Nothing had changed. I didn't get to the top that time, but stayed at the side, and really got a good look at it.

It was resting on a steep ledge of bluish-green rock about 3,000 feet wide.

Another thing I noticed was that I didn't see any nails at all. It seemed that the whole ship was made of one piece of petrified wood.

There was definitely no door in the side of the ship that I could see. No opening of any kind. There may have been one in the part I couldn't see, but that I don't know. That side was practically inaccessible. I could only see my side and part of the bow.

The sides were slanting outward to the top and the front was flat too. I didn't see any real curves. It was unlike any other boat I have ever seen. It looked more like a flat-bottomed barge.

The Hagopian account has provided enough details for artist-interviewer Elfred Lee to sketch a likeness of the ark. Hagopian approved the final sketch, which has since been published in several magazines and Biblical references. Also his account has given us some valuable information concerning the Ark's windows and the holes in the roof, which we'll discuss in Chapter 8 when we analyze the Ark.

The next reported sighting of the Ark was in 1916, when two Russian aviators saw the remains of the ancient vessel while flying over the slopes of Mt. Ararat.

Ark Seen From Air

Pilot Vladimir Roskovitsky was interviewed after World War I by Robert Anderson, a member of the Mormon Church. The aviator had fled Russia shortly after the Bolshevik Revolution.

Here's the story in Roskovitsky's own words:

It was just before the Russian Revolution that this story really began. A group of Russian aviators were stationed at a lonely temporary outpost about twenty-five miles northeast of Mount Ararat. The day was hot and dry as August days so often are in this semidesert land.

Far up on the side of the mountain we could see a thunder shower, while still further up we could see the white snowcaps of Mount Ararat. Just then the captain walked in and announced that plane number seven had its new supercharger installed and was ready for high altitude tests and ordered my buddy and me to make the test.

102

At least we could escape from the heat! We wasted no time in getting our parachutes strapped on, our oxygen cans, and completing other required tasks that needed doing before the assigned flight. Then we climbed into the cockpit, fastened our safety belts, and we were in the air.

Circling the field several times until we reached the 14,-000 foot mark, we stopped climbing for a few minutes to become accustomed to the altitude. I looked to the right to the beautiful snow-capped mountains. Twenty-six miles is a short distance when flying at a speed of 100 miles per hour. After circling several times around the snow-capped cone, we made a long, swift glide down the slope and suddenly came upon a perfect lake.

We returned for another look and suddenly my companion observed something and excitedly pointed to the overflow of the lake. We thought it a submarine, but on looking closer we saw that it had a stubby mast, the top was rounded over, with a flat catwalk about five feet wide down the length of it. What a strange craft, built as though the designer had expected the waves to roll over the top most of the time and had engineered it to wallow in the sea like a log . . . .

We flew down as far as safety permitted and took several circles around it. When we got close to it, we were surprised to discover the size of it, for it was as long as a city block and would compare favorably in size with a modern battleship of this day.

It was grounded on the shores of the lake with about one-fourth of the hull under water. It had been partly dismantled on one side near the front and on the other side there were great doorways, one nearly twenty-four feet square, but the door was gone. This seemed quite out of proportion, as even today, ships seldom have doors even half that large.

Roskovitsky returned to base and reported his discovery to the captain, who asked to be flown to the site.

"This strange craft," the captain said, "is Noah's Ark!

It has been sitting at 14,000 feet for 5,000 years, being frozen nine or ten months, perhaps longer, in a year. It has been in cold storage, as it were, all this time. You have made the most amazing discovery of the age."

Czar Sends Soldiers

Roskovitsky's account of the events continues:

When the captain sent this report to the Russian government it aroused considerable interest, which resulted in the Czar's sending two special companies of soldiers to climb the mountain. One group of 100 men attacked the mountain from the other side. Two weeks of hard labor was required to chop out a trail along the cliffs of the lower part of the mountain, and it was nearly a month before the Ark was reached.

Complete measurements of it were taken, plans drawn of it, and numerous photographs were made, all of which were sent to the Czar. The Ark was found to contain hundreds of small rooms, some with very high ceilings. Some unusually large rooms had fences of great timbers across them, some of which were two feet thick and designed to hold beasts ten times as large as elephants. Other rooms were lined with cages reminding us of those used in poultry shows, only instead of chicken wire there were rows of iron or metal bars across the front.

Everything was heavily painted with a warlike paint resembling shellac and the workmanship of the craft showed all signs of a high type of civilization. The wood used throughout was similar to the cypress family which never rots, and which, being painted and frozen most of the time, accounts for its condition of perfect preservation.

Only a few days after the report was sent to the Czar, the Russian government was overthrown by the Bolshevik Revolution and no doubt the records were destroyed—at least they were never made public—in an effort of Bolshevism to discredit all belief in the truth of the Bible.

The White Russians of the air fleet escaped through Armenia where we could be free to live according to the Good Book. . . .

Critics say that while the facts of this account are true, the story has been embellished.

"I've learned there was a contingent of Russian airmen stationed at the foot of the mountain in 1917. They did fly their planes around and over Mount Ararat; they fled the Armenian area when they heard of the overthrow of the Czar; and several members of the unit are known to have made their way to the United States," says Dallas radio commentator Melvin Munn, who admits that he has not been able to verify any of the specific details of the Roskovitsky account. "Neither have we found solid research reasons to discredit or disbelieve the account."[1]

Story Verified

Eryl Cummings did extensive research on this story to determine its authenticity. He obtained verifications from relatives and acquaintances of soldiers who were actually on the expedition. And he confirmed information from the author of the original Russian article (published in *Rosseya*, November, 1945), which was the basis for the presumably exaggerated popular accounts.

The article was written by Col. Alexander A. Koor, an officer in the Czar's White Russian Army and a friend of some of the soldiers involved in the reconnaissance expedition.

Cummings received the following communication from Koor on March 1, 1946, concerning the existence of Russian troops in the Ararat area:

The headquarters of the 14th Railroad Battalion was at Bayazit, just southwest of Greater Ararat, with Brigade Headquarters at Maku, southeast of Lesser Ararat, commanded by Col. Sverczkoff. The 14th Battalion came to the front in the summer of 1916 from Russia. I understand that the discovery of Noah's Ark was in the end of 1916, with the scouting parties having to wait until the summer of 1917.

I know that Sergeant Boris V. Rujansky belonged to the 14th Battalion. I understand, and it is logical, that the first and second parties of the expedition to Mount Ararat were formed from the local force of the 14th Battalion or 3-D Zamorsky Brigade, by order from the local Brigade Headquarters. . . .

In 1916 the 3-D Caucasian Aviation Detachment, under the command of 1st Lt. Zabolotsky,* served air duty over the region at Mount Ararat, Lake Van and Lake Urmia. This aviation detachment served the 4th Caucasian Corps, and the Army Aviation Inspector was Captain Koorbatoff. I hope 1st Lt. Zabolotsky is the man you are looking for, for he, from an airplane, sighted the Ark and started the investigation. Captain Koorbatoff was his supervisor . . .[2]

Koor also provided Cummings with the following statement about the Russian expedition:

TO WHOM IT MAY CONCERN; This is to certify that I, Alexander A. Koor, former colonel and Chief-in-Command of the 19th Petropaulovsky Regiment, heard the following concerning the discovery of Noah's Ark:

(1) 1st Lt. Paul Vasilivich Rujansky of the 156th El-isavetpolsky regiment, Caucasian Army. I knew all of Rujansky's family for years. I met them in the city of Kazan, Russia, where I attended the government military academy. 1st Lt. Rujansky was wounded in Erzerum when his regiment took Chaban Dede, central fort of the Erzerum fortifications. He was relieved from active duty and sent to work in the Commandant's office, in the city of Irkustsk, Siberia. After the Bolsheviks made an uprising, he moved to the city of Harbin, Manchuria, where I found him in 1921.

* *Authors' Note*—Zabolotsky and Valdimir Roskovitsky may be the same individual or Zabolotsky may have been Roskovitsky's flight companion during the flight when the Ark was discovered.

Known as the "Nampa Image", this female clay doll was found in a flood-laid sedimentary deposit at a depth of 300 feet while boring for an artesian well in Nampa, Idaho in 1889. Whoever made the doll had lived there or it was washed there by flood action. In Genesis 7 and 8, the deluge buried the pre-Flood civilizations encasing fossils and artifacts alike in what are now the sedimentary layers of the Earth's crust.

GEORGE ZAPPLER

Thousands of vertebrate animals, insects, molluscs and plants were found in the lignite beds of Geiseltal, Germany. These fossils of animals and plants from all climatic zones of the world contained well-preserved bits of hair, feathers and scales. Such preservation could only take place through very rapid incrustation which flood geologists believe occurred during the universal Flood recorded in the Bible. Pictured is a crocodile fossil from the Geiseltal lignite bed.

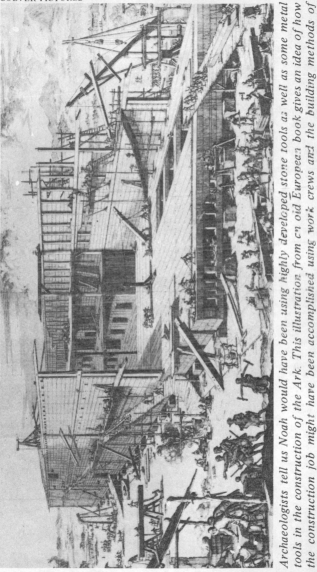

Archaeologists tell us Noah would have been using highly developed stone tools as well as some metal tools in the construction of the Ark. This illustration from an old European book gives an idea of how the construction job might have been accomplished using work crews and the building methods of Noah's day.

Noah and his workers are hoisting one of the structural beams into place during a reenactment scene of Noah building the Ark, in Sun Classic Pictures' "In Search of Noah's Ark." The Biblical Noah built the real Ark 450 feet long, 75 feet wide and 45 feet high. It contained three 14-foot high decks, divided into stalls and cages for housing animals.

Elaborate planning goes into the shooting of every scene in a motion picture. About to take place is a scene where Noah takes a break from Ark building tasks to eat and talk with his family. "In Search of Noah's Ark," required a cast of 71 people plus many stand-in performers.

Noah with one of the animals taken aboard the Ark during a scene from "In Search of Noah's Ark." Nearly 30 different kinds of animals were used in the docu-drama. However, scientists believe the real Noah took between 628 and 800 kinds of animals aboard his Ark more than 5,000 years ago.

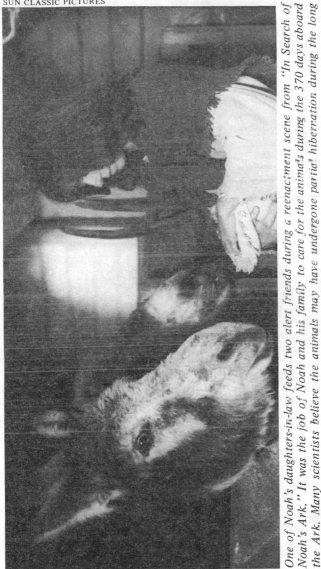

One of Noah's daughters-in-law feeds two alert friends during a reenactment scene from "In Search of Noah's Ark." It was the job of Noah and his family to care for the animals during the 370 days aboard the Ark. Many scientists believe the animals may have undergone partial hibernation during the long voyage.

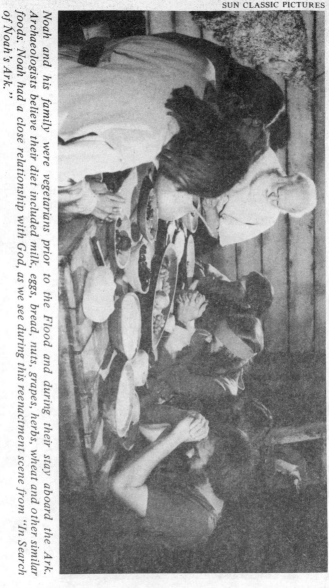

Noah and his family were vegetarians prior to the Flood and during their stay aboard the Ark. Archaeologists believe their diet included milk, eggs, bread, nuts, grapes, herbs, wheat and other similar foods. Noah had a close relationship with God, as we see during this reenactment scene from "In Search of Noah's Ark."

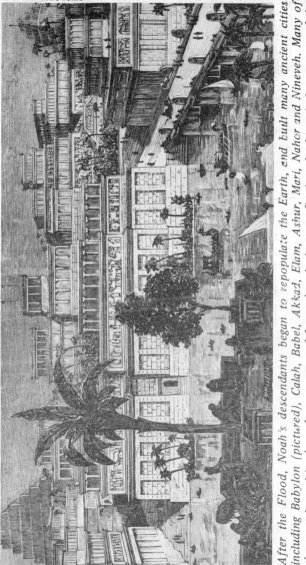

After the Flood, Noah's descendants began to repopulate the Earth, and built many ancient cities including Babylon (pictured), Calah, Babel, Akkad, Elam, Ashur, Mari, Nahor and Nineveh. Many of these ancient cities have been excavated by archaeologists, confirming the historical accuracy of the Bible.

Genesis 11:1-9 mentions the building of a multi-storied Tower of Babel. It was the first such tower attempted, and a symbol of man's rebellion against God according to the Genesis account. It stands in the town of Borsippa, a few miles south of the ruins of Babylon in Iraq. Although it is a roost for pigeons today, it does attest to the historical accuracy of the Bible.

"Believe It or Not" columnist Robert Ripley, who has never been proved wrong, found the authentic tomb of Noah in the Lebanon mountains of the Holy Land near the ancient city of Damascus. It is a very sacred spot as shown by the gifts of clothing and shawls brought to the tomb. Ripley is seated in the foreground.

Researcher Robert Ripley is dwarfed as he poses for a picture beside the anchors from Noah's Ark in Kairouan, Tunisia. Ripley says these very anchors were used in tying the Ark to Mt. Ararat. No one has yet been able to refute his claim or offer any alternative explanation for the anchors.

Following the flood, the Ark came to rest on the slopes of Mt. Ararat in Eastern Turkey, according to the Bible. Ark explorers have discovered Ararat to be a very treacherous mountain with storms and blizzards occurring practically every day. Although a storm is building up over the summit, the south face of Mt. Ararat looks quite serene from a distance. Conversations between climbers can set off rock or snow avalanches, which have been fatal to some climbers. Pictured is an Ararat rock avalanche in progress.

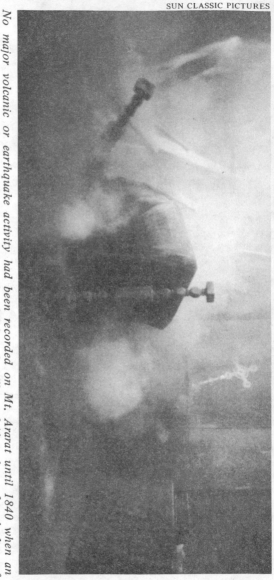

No major volcanic or earthquake activity had been recorded on Mt. Ararat until 1840 when an earthquake and volcanic rupture covered with mud and debris the village of Ahora located at the base of the mountain. The upheaval destroyed the 800 year old St. Jacob's Monastery which had housed numerous Ark relics. From the film, "In Search of Noah's Ark," the photo shows a reenactment of this earthquake destroying the monastery.

The first person to reach the Ararat summit in recorded times was a Russian born, German physician named Dr. Friedrich W. Parrot. A professor at the University of Dorpat in Russia, Dr. Parrot reached the summit in 1829. This picture was taken during a reenactment scene of the expedition from "In Search of Noah's Ark."

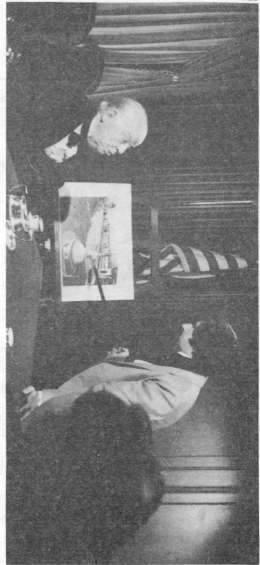

In 1887, Prince John Joseph Nouri, found the Ark on Mt. Ararat wedged in rocks and half-filled with ice and snow. Prince Nouri came to the U.S. in hopes of interesting potential investors in forming an expedition to excavate the Ark, with the idea of exhibiting it at the 1893 World's Fair in Chicago. This photo was taken of Nouri making an appeal to potential investors during a reenactment scene from "In Search of Noah's Ark."

One of the 20th Century's most detailed descriptions of what the Ark looks like was furnished by George Hagopian, who was taken to the Ark on Mt. Ararat by his uncle in 1902. In a 1970 interview, Hagopian said that he actually walked on the roof of the Ark. In a reenactment scene from "In Search of Noah's Ark," we see Hagopian as a boy with his uncle building a "rock ladder" beside the Ark.

Russian aviator Vladimir Roskovitsky spotted the Ark while flying around Mt. Ararat in 1916. A year later a reconnaissance expedition composed of about 100 Russian soldiers arrived at the site and took complete measurements and photos. The material was sent to the Czar, but was lost during the Russian Revolution. This photo was taken of Russian soldiers studying the Ark during a reenactment scene from "In Search of Noah's Ark."

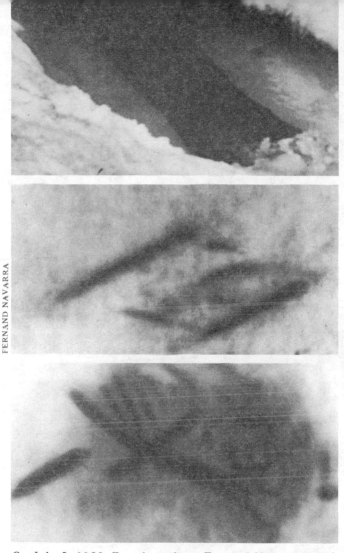

On July 5, 1955, French explorer Fernand Navarra neared the bottom of a crevasse on Mt. Ararat where he barely had enough light to shoot these photos of beams under the icy water. These beams photographed from above the water's surface at the bottom of a 35-foot crevasse on a treeless Mt. Ararat are fragments from the Ark according to Navarra.

Navarra descends vertically into the crevasse where the Ark lies about 35 feet below. When Navarra got near the bottom he realized there was not enough daylight left in the afternoon to attempt a safe recovery of wood on that day. He feared blocks of ice might break off and trap him below.

Following the discovery of the crevasse, a sudden snow storm hit forcing Navarra and his son to seek refuge for the night inside an igloo-like ice cave. The next day Navarra again descended into the snow covered crevasse and cut off a beam. In the photo, 12-year old Raphael pulls the heavy dark beam out of the crevasse. The crescent-shaped right side is where it was disconnected from a longer subterranean beam.

On July 6, 1955, Fernand Navarra posed atop the crevasse where he recovered a piece of wood believed to be from Noah's Ark. This moment was the apex of his three expeditions to Mt. Ararat in search of Noah's Ark.

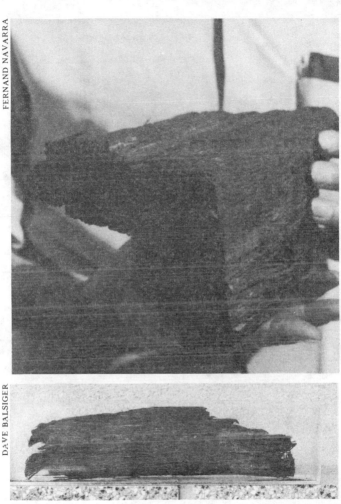

Navarra holds a piece of the recovered structural beam which has been both hand hewn and squared. The bottom photo shows a piece of wood recovered by Navarra during the 1969 SEARCH Foundation expedition. It is believed to be planking from the Ark and is encased in a special container to prevent deterioration.

Based on the 1902 sighting of the Ark by George Hagopian, artist-illustrator Elfred Lee drew this picture to match Hagopian's description of the ancient vessel. Scientists tell us the barge-like Ark was one of the most stable vessels ever built and particularly well designed for floating out the flood.

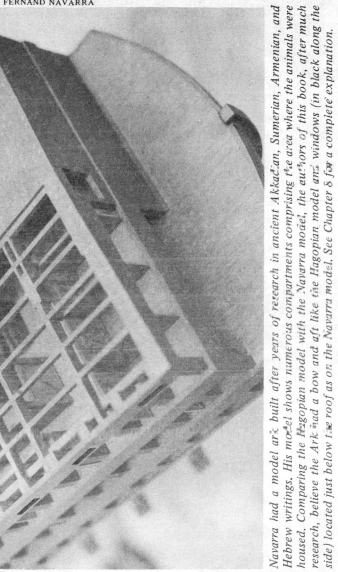

Navarra had a model ark built after years of research in ancient Akkadian, Sumerian, Armenian, and Hebrew writings. His model shows numerous compartments comprising the area where the animals were housed. Comparing the Hagopian model with the Navarra model, the authors of this book, after much research, believe the Ark had a bow and aft like the Hagopian model and windows (in black along the side) located just below the roof as on the Navarra model. See Chapter 8 for a complete explanation.

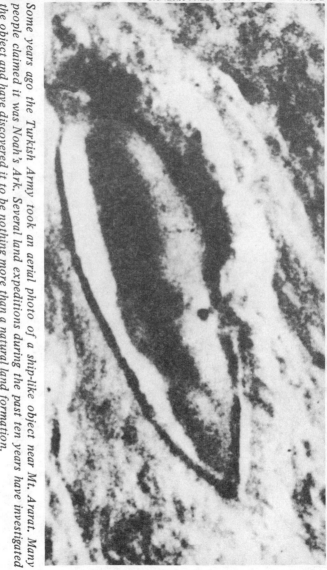

Some years ago the Turkish Army took an aerial photo of a ship-like object near Mt. Ararat. Many people claimed it was Noah's Ark. Several land expeditions during the past ten years have investigated the object and have discovered it to be nothing more than a natural land formation.

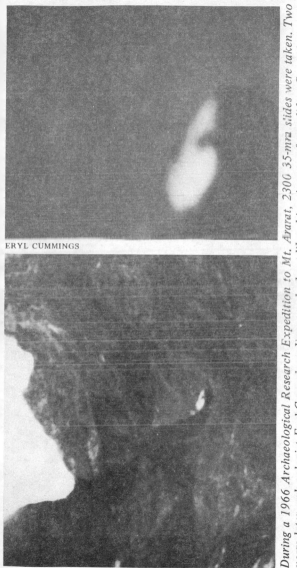

ERYL CUMMINGS

During a 1966 Archaeological Research Expedition to Mt. Ararat, 2306 35-mm slides were taken. Two years later, ark-eologist Eryl Cummings discovered a boat-like object in one of the slides. Cummings says the area needs to be explored to determine if the object is in fact the Ark or just a huge boulder. The photo on the right is a blow-up of the unidentified object.

The Holy Ground Changing Center, a religious commune based in Frankston, Texas, says they took this photo with a telephoto lens on Mt. Ararat in 1974. They say it shows the Ark (bow in the upper right) on a ledge with the planking on the Ark's side clearly visible. Many serious Ark researchers question whether the photo is genuine. Some critics contend that the photo has been retouched. Only further expeditions will solve this mystery.

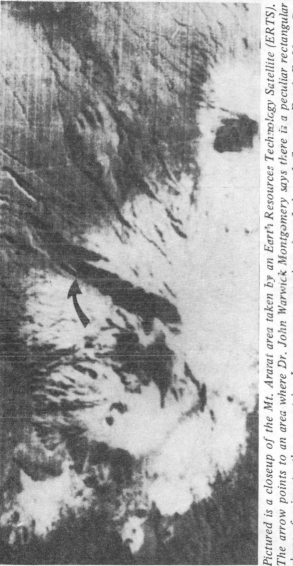

Pictured is a closeup of the Mt. Ararat area taken by an Earth Resources Technology Satellite (ERTS). The arrow points to an area where Dr. John Warwick Montgomery says there is a peculiar rectangular shape, foreign to the mountain. In newspaper stories released through Senator Frank E. Moss, Dr. Montgomery speculates that the rectangle is Noah's Ark. However, most NASA officials contend that ERTS was not capable of photographing something as small as the Ark.

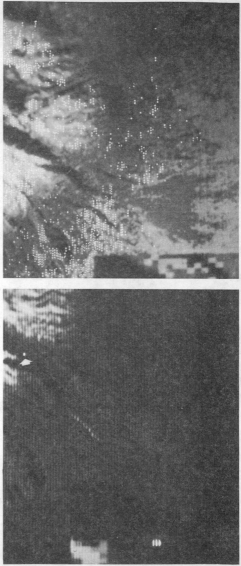

These photos show an electronic computer data analysis of the suspected Ark location, as conducted at the Earth Resources Observation Satellite Center in Sioux Falls, South Dakota. The many areas which are illuminated (small dots) indicate that this particular suspected area is NOT the Ark location, but a typical section of the mountain. The single illuminated area indicates that this particular section of land has a reflective pattern different from any of the surrounding area. Could it be the Ark's location? It is near the area of Dr. Montgomery's mysterious rectangle and close to where Navarra found his wood.

U.S. DEPARTMENT OF THE INTERIOR
GEOLOGICAL SURVEY

Could the Ark really have survived the huge waves of a universal flood? We decided to test a model ark built to the same proportions as the Biblical Ark to obtain our answer. The tests conducted in southern California by an internationally known hydraulics lab disclosed that the Ark could have easily survived a 200-foot wave without capsizing. The Ark had a tendency to naturally propel its bow into the waves. The photo shows the model ark in a wave tank overtaking a wave which would be equivalent to a 200-foot ocean wave.

The Ark remained the largest, most stable vessel ever built until its size and ratio were almost duplicated in 1844 by the ship Great Britain. Although in ancient Egypt, Queen Hatshepsut built a wider ship than the Ark, it wasn't until 1884 that a vessel — the Etruria, a Cunard liner — was built longer than the Ark. Pictured we see the Ark during a reenactment scene from "In Search of Noah's Ark."

(2) Lt. Peter Nicolovich Leslin of the 261st Ahilchinsky regiment, also of the Caucasian Army. During the Bolshevik uprising he was arrested, but escaped, and in December 1918 he joined my Petropaulovsky regiment.

(3) About July or August 1921, I and Lt. Leslin met 1st Lt. Rujansky in Harbin. During one of our conversations, 1st Lt. Rujansky told me about the discovery of Noah's Ark. He didn't know about the details because he was wounded and sent to Russia, but he knew because his brother, Boris Vasilivich Rujansky, Sergeant of the Military Railroad Battalion, was a member of the investigating party which was sent to Mount Ararat to corroborate the discovery of Noah's Ark.

Lt. Leslin admitted he had also heard about the discovery of Noah's Ark, not as a rumor, but as news, from the Senior Adjutant of his division, who had told him that Noah's Ark was found in the saddle of two peaks of Mount Ararat.
This is all I heard from these two officers, and I am sure both told me the truth.

(Signed) Col. Alexander A. Koor[8]

Koor thus verified the basic facts of the Roskovitsky story. Critics, however, were skeptical. They asked, why did Koor wait until 1945 to submit his knowledge about the location of the Ark. And judging from the *Rosseya* account, they said, his knowledge of the Russian discovery was quite detailed—too detailed for someone who had heard it from casual acquaintances. They suspicioned he had copied and embellished the story from a similar account published in the *New Eden Magazine* in 1940.

Colonel Koor's Credibility

But while critics were busy tearing down Koor's credibility, Ark researcher Dr. John Montgomery decided to interview Koor himself.

Dr. Montgomery visited him in the spring of 1970,

spending an afternoon with him and his daughter in their book-filled apartment in Menlo Park, California. (Koor has since passed away.)

"I had no doubt of the Colonel's integrity and scholarly precision in conveying factual data," Dr. Montgomery says. "He in turn, was fully confident of his sources, having known intimately the officers who gave him accounts of their sightings of the Ark on Ararat.[4]

"The author of the *Rosseya* article, Colonel Alexander A. Koor, was formerly a White Russian Army officer under the Czar, who had been in command of troops in the Ararat area during the closing years of the First World War," Dr. Montgomery continues. "He had also fought against the Bolsheviks, finally escaping with his wife into Manchuria, eventually reaching asylum in the United States.

"Koor's military background and service in the area around Mount Ararat provided ample evidence of his qualifications as author of the *Rosseya* story, since he had personally known relatives of some of the members of the land expedition who investigated the reported discovery of the Ark."[5]

Russian Airmen Visit

The authors of this book pursued the investigation further by locating Mrs. Gladys Evans, an El Cajon, California, resident who remembers that three of the White Russian airmen who had flown over the Ark in 1916 and had been on the 1917 foot reconnaissance expedition, spent a week in her father's San Bernardino, California, home as house guests in the fall of 1940.

Mrs. Evans vividly remembers some of the details described by the airmen to her father and brother:

They told how the Ark was "half in and half out of a lake like a log floating in water. It was an immense thing, and it had cages—some with metal on them. It had a catwalk on top and the door was off. The door was near by and had apparently been struck by lightning because it was partly burnt. The Ark was pitched within and without with some kind of lacquer. It was just as good as the day it was built." The wood reminded them of oleander.

When they first saw the Ark from the air, they thought it was a submarine, but couldn't figure out why someone would be building it on a mountain. On the later reconnaissance expedition these three airmen actually got inside the Ark where they took pictures and measurements. The film was turned over to the Russian government.[6]

The Russian airmen who stayed at the home of Mrs. Evans' father were not the same airmen who first spotted the Ark while testing their airplane. Mrs. Evans says these airmen also flew around the site, but the original discoverers were other Russian airman whose names, mentioned at the time, have since been forgotten by Mrs. Evans.

Our research generally confirms the fact that many of the White Russians who saw the Ark from the air or on the reconnaissance expedition escaped Russia and made their way to America. All agree on the basic facts that the Ark was discovered by aviators and later an expedition was sent to study the vessel.

If there is any embellishment of the general account, it's because each eye witness, in telling his own version of the discovery, has no doubt told it as he remembered it, emphasizing details which were significant to him as an observer.

We have presented descriptions of the Ark from the observations of George Hagopian and the Russian aviators. But has science been able to tell us anything about the construction of the Ark?

Where was it built? How was it built? What were its dimensions? How long did the construction take? Answers to these questions will shed a lot more light on solving the mystery of Noah's Ark.

Footnotes
Chapter 7

1. Munn, Melvin, "Noah's Ark", Life Line Freedom Talk, May 24, 1971, No. 44.
2. Cummings, Violet M., *Noah's Ark: Fact or Fable?* (Creation-Science Research Center, San Diego, CA, 1971) pp. 143-144.
3. *Ibid.*, pp. 144-145.
4. Montgomery, John Warwick, *The Quest for Noah's Ark* (Bethany Fellowship, Inc., Minneapolis, MN, 1972) p. 245.
5. *Ibid.*, pp. 115-116.
6. Interview with Gladys Evans in February 1976, El Cajon, California.

CHAPTER 8

A Thorough Analysis of Noah's Ark

Artists for the last 2,000 years have had many different ideas of what the Ark looked like. It's been pictured as a prismatic rhomboid, pregnant sampan, great hulled vessel, and as a sailing ship. It has seldom been pictured by artists as it really appeared—a rather ugly, barge-like rectangular box. But how do we know what it looked like?

Well, God talked directly with Noah and told him how to build the Ark. Those who believe in God have no difficulty believing that God could and would communicate with Noah. The Bible constantly asserts that this happens.

In some cases God speaks to people in visions (Isaiah, Ezekiel, Daniel), to others in dreams (Pharaoh, Nebuchadnezzar), and to others by a voice which they hear (Samuel, Saul of Tarsus, John the Apostle). We may conclude that Noah heard a voice telling him what to do, and it's very possible that God revealed or illustrated to him in a vision the type of vessel required.

Exactly how did God tell Noah to build the Ark? In Genesis 6:14-16, God gives Noah the following instructions:

Make yourself an ark of gopherwood, put various compartments in it, and cover it inside and out with pitch. This is how you shall build it: the length of the ark shall be three hundred cubits, its width fifty cubits, and its height thirty cubits. Make an opening for daylight in the ark, and finish the ark a cubit above it. Put an entrance in the side of the ark, which you shall make with bottom, second and third decks. (*The New American Bible*-Catholic version)

111

Was Job Impossible?

A point that has concerned many critics of the Biblical Ark account is whether ancient man could have undertaken such a massive construction job which may have taken up to 100 years to complete.

Dr. Frederick A. Filby, British scientist and member of the Palestine and Egypt Exploration Societies, says "It seems reasonable, on the natural level, to suppose that Noah possessed that constructive genius which manifests itself from time to time throughout history in the construction of something far beyond the achievement of a man's contemporaries.

"It was surely the type of genius shown by Imhotep in the design of the Step Pyramid, by the architect of the Hanging Gardens of Babylon, by Ictinus and Callicrates in the building of the Parthenon, and by Chares of Lindus in the construction of the Colossus of Rhodes.

"If we reject the story (of Noah building the Ark), and say that the task was too great, and that no man could have stood out so far ahead of his contemporaries, then we must reject the other seven wonders of the ancient world. Noah was only the first of that line of geniuses who designed and constructed something which far outshone the capacity of their contemporaries."[1]

God told Noah to build the ark 300 by 50 by 30 cubits. Let's picture that size.

In ancient times the cubit was the distance between an average man's elbow and fingertips, which ranged from about 18 to 22 inches long. Using the smallest measure —the one most frequently used by the ancient Hebrew people—we can say that Noah's Ark was 450 feet long, 75 feet wide and 45 feet high. It resembled a long rectangular box.

It was the largest wooden vessel ever built by man in any age. Its roof area was larger than 20 college basketball courts.

Under any consideration, the Ark was a very large boat. Some critics have also suggested that the Biblical

Ark was beyond the capability of boat building craftsmen of ancient times.

But regardless of what the critics say, there is a giant boat-like artifact embedded in the ice on the upper slopes of Mt. Ararat. The logical conclusion—man was not only capable of building it, but did build it!

Yet evidence does exist that early man undertook major boat building projects. Archaeologists have pictures of boats, including one with a steering oar, belonging to *pre*-dynastic times in Egypt.[2] From the time of Menes, First Dynasty, we have a palette with a finely carved picture of a high-prowed boat. It is believed that the very early Egyptians and Phoenicians sailed out over the Mediterranean and there is an account of Pharaoh Snofru[3] (3rd Dynasty) sending forty ships to Byblos to buy cedar wood for shipbuilding. In Snofru's thirteenth year of reign a ship of 100 cubits in length was built as well as 60 lesser ships. There also are references to boats of the Middle Kingdom of Egypt with crews of 120 men.

The most interesting vessels of ancient Egypt were those used for transporting giant obelisks down the Nile. An Egyptian official, Ineri, reports that in the time of Thothmes I, he had a vessel built for the transport of two obelisks, which together weighed about 350 tons. The vessel was 120 cubits long by 40 cubits wide (180 feet by 60 feet).

But Queen Hatshepsut had a much larger vessel—200 feet by 80 feet—designed to transport two great obelisks, which weighed 350 tons each. Her boat weighed about 800 tons and with its load, 1,500 tons. *This boat was wider than the Ark*—nearly as wide as the Lusitania.[4]

These ancient ships were made of very thick, smoothed timbers often a foot thick. The beams were fastened together at regular intervals by special pieces of wood shaped like a letter X, and the joints were then sealed with bitumen pitch. Other members were held by wooden pegs and by such means longitudinal and cross-walls and struts could be inserted and fastened to the main structure. Copper saws up to 16 inches long, dowels, and pegs

113

can be found in First Dynasty references and even earlier. Mortise and tenon joints and dove-tailing also were used by ancient ship builders to keep their structures together.[5]

Metal Tools Available

Since the Ark was built before pre-Dynastic times, the question arises as to the tools Noah used. Were they stone or metal?

According to the Bible, Tubal-cain was a forger of bronze and iron before the Flood. Thus metal tools would have been available in Noah's time. As a matter of fact, the Bereshith Rabba Jewish tradition says that Naamah, the sister of Tubal-cain, was Noah's wife. If Naamah was the wife of Noah, it would mean that Noah, being related to Tubal-cain, surely would have had access to metal tools. However, we must admit that nothing can be concluded for certain from this Jewish tradition.

But let's speculate that Noah may have been restricted to stone age tools. Could he have done the job?

In a book entitled, *The Neolithic Revolution*, by Sonia Cole, we see a picture of a Danish workman cutting down a tree with an ancient polished stone axe. Three workmen cleared 600 square yards of birch forest in four hours using these tools. One of the stone age axes, which had not been sharpened for 4,000 years, was used to fell 100 trees. In addition to the axe, ancient man used the adze for smoothing his beams and saws for cutting. The British Museum has a pre-Dynastic flint saw which still looks very efficient.

Now that we have covered some of the feasibility aspects of building the Ark, let's compare it to modern day ships.

Shipbuilders have discovered that the Ark's length to breadth equals a ratio of 6 to 1, *meaning it would be a slow moving vessel.*

In 1604, a Dutch merchant, Peter Jansen, had a boat built at Hoorn, 120 by 20 by 12 feet—exactly the same ratio as the Ark. The vessel proved to be admirably suited for carrying freight. It is said that several vessels with the same proportions were built in Denmark.[6]

The Ark remained the largest, most stable boat ever built until its size and ratio were almost duplicated in 1844 by the *Great Britain*. That ship was only slightly smaller than the Ark, measuring 322 by 51 by 32 ½ feet. The designer, I. K. Brunel, had the accumulated knowledge of generations of shipbuilders, but the Ark was the first of its kind.[7]

A number of modern vessels designed for speed have a mean ratio of 8.1 to 1. Examples of this ratio would be the *Queen Elizabeth* with a ratio of 8.6 to 1, or the *Canberra* with a ratio of 8.2 to 1. Modern, slower-moving, oil tankers are quite similar to the Ark with a ratio of 7 to 1.[8]

Design Was Sound

Dr. Henry Morris, a former professor of hydraulic engineering at Virginia Polytechnic Institute, says the proportions of the Ark in length, breadth and depth have been proven to be hydrodynamically sound.

The Ark design ratio also means greater capacity, greater safety in operation, and a smaller crew. It was distinctly designed to "float" out the Flood. If it had been designed in the shape of a square cube instead of its rectangular shape, the Ark would have gone into a constant spin, creating disastrous conditions aboard the vessel.

It wasn't until 1884 that a vessel— the *Eturia,* a Cunard liner—was built longer than the Ark.

By comparison, the *Queen Mary*, now a floating museum in Long Beach, California, is a little more than twice the length of the Ark at 1018 feet.[9]

With the Ark's dimensions of 450 × 75 × 45 feet, and taken as a rectangular box, the total volume of the Ark would be 1,518,750 cubic feet. It would take about 280,000 cubic feet of timber—between 9,000 to 13,000 planks—to construct the boat, which has been estimated at a little more than 4,100 tons dead weight.[10]

With ocean water figured at 35 cubic feet per ton, the Ark, completely empty, would float with its bottom about 4.3 feet below water. Loading it to where it would sink to a depth of 15 feet would require 10,000 tons of cargo, and to 20 feet, 15,000 tons. Assuming the weight of the animals as 100 tons, and allowing each animal 20 times its own weight of food and 20 times its weight of water for a year, the cargo would weigh about 4,000 tons. We don't know, of course, how many tons of animals were aboard, but these calculations are within reason and extremely conservative.

The Ark was large enough to have carried more cargo than 569 railroad freight cars—each car contains 2,670 cubic feet—or up to 30,000 animals and birds, with lots of room left over for Noah and his family.

Great Stability

Like the giant vessels of today, the Ark's lower center of gravity gave it a tremendous stability. The lower it sank in the water due to its heavy cargo, the more stable it became.

Marine experts agree that Noah's Ark could have remained seaworthy indefinitely, even in the most severe storms.

Dr. Morris says, "In the complex of hydrodynamic and aerodynamic forces unleashed in the Flood, it was necessary that the Ark remain afloat for a whole year.

"In addition to floating, it must not capsize under the impact of the great waves and winds that might beat against it. The Bible says the floodwaters rose at least 15 cubits above the highest mountains (Gen. 7:20) evidently to point out that the Ark was floating freely wherever the waters might propel it.

"The height of the Ark was 30 cubits, so it seems probable that the 15 cubit (22.5 feet) figure represents the draft of the Ark when loaded. When the Ark was floating at this depth, Archimedes' principle tells us that its weight must have equalled the force of buoyancy, which in turn

116

equals the weight of the equivalent amount of water displaced.

"Fresh water weighs 62.4 lbs. and sea water 64 lbs. per cubic foot. Because of the minerals and sediments in the water, its density may well have been at least that of sea water, in which case the total loaded weight of the Ark would be calculated at 48,600,000 pounds (24,300 tons).

"The average unit weight of the Ark must then be half that of the water, or 32 lbs. per cubic foot. The center of gravity of the Ark and its contents presumably would be close to its geometric center, with the framework, the animals, and other contents more or less uniformly and symmetrically dispersed throughout the structure."

Dr. Morris concludes that the Ark's construction would have made it impossible to capsize, even in the middle of heavy waves and violent winds.

"The Ark as designed," he says, "was highly stable, admirable suited for its purpose of riding out the storms of the year of the great Flood."[11]

Modern Danish barges, called fleuten, are miniature counterparts of the Ark. On a smaller scale, they demonstrate what must have been the Ark's capacity and stability.

Built to the Ark's proportions, these barges could carry more than the more conventionally shaped vessels. Like the Ark, they are almost impossible to capsize.

Tests Prove Ark's Stability

While making the motion picture "In Search of Noah's Ark," we decided to spend several thousand dollars to test a model ark built to the same proportions as the Biblical Ark. We wanted to test the various stability theories as modern ship builders do when designing and building new ocean going vessels.

We had our tests conducted in southern California by an internationally known hydraulics laboratory which asked us to not disclose its name.

The following interview was conducted with the hydraulics lab project test director after the testing:

Q. *How high a wave could the Ark have survived?*

117

A. The tests showed that the Ark could survive waves higher than you would ever encounter in the ocean.

Q. What is the maximum height of a wave the Ark could have survived based on your test results?

A. More than a 200-foot wave without capsizing. But there are no waves that large in the ocean.

Q. What about tidal waves—would they ever be high enough to capsize the Ark?

A. A peaked up tidal wave could maybe reach 100 feet or more—but this would happen only close to shore in shallow water, not in the ocean.

Q. Then because of the Ark's unique design ratio, it could have survived any type of wave produced by the ocean?

A. If it were hit broadside by a gigantic wave, it's conceivable that it could have been capsized. However, the surprising thing revealed by the tests was that the Ark naturally propelled its bow into the waves. It's a remarkably stable vessel.

A Place For Everything

The Ark had three decks, each about 14 feet high, if we allow a foot for the thick floor planking and assume only a slight slope of the roof. The Ark was evidently divided longways and crossways into compartments or rooms, according to the Bible.

It would be probable that at least two long dividing walls would run the length of the ship, making a central passageway with rooms or pens on either side. If the central passageway were about 15 feet wide, this would give us siderooms or pens up to a horizontal depth of 30 feet—although we suspect many of these larger pens would have been partitioned into smaller ones. Actually, no one really knows how Noah planned out his compartments, nor whether he built them on each deck. Our speculations can only be based on commonly known husbandry practices used in the caring and housing of animals.

118

The compartment walls were not only important in keeping the animals separated, but the large wall beams provided the necessary internal strength to keep the Ark sturdy. "This Ark had firm walls and a roof, and was braced with cross beams," wrote Josephus, the Jewish historian in his book *Antiquities of the Jews.*

Also, the Ark no doubt contained granaries where the food for both animals and Noah's family were stored. To believe that Noah, who must have been an expert carpenter, planned and constructed a number of granaries in the Ark would not be difficult. The space between decks was about 15 feet—very similar to the height of the Egyptian granaries of the sixth Dynasty.

Wooden stairs or a sloping ramp would have connected each deck. Open "portholes" and windows that could be closed also existed in the Ark.

Charles A. Totten, professor of military science and tactics at Yale University, has compiled some interesting figures. The three decks contained a total of 101,250 square feet of space, or 33,750 square feet per deck. He suggests that the small and medium-sized animals were put in cages, in tiers, one above the other, since the cubic space must be considered as well as floor space.

Some animal husbandry experts believe the top floor was occupied by Noah's family, food stuffs, and bird cages. The second deck probably contained granaries, rows of pens for housing larger animals and tiers of cages for keeping the smaller animals separate. The bottom deck is believed to have been used primarily for waste storage.

Dr. Filby has a different view of how the animals, people and food stuffs were arranged in the Ark. Noah, his family and the living creatures lived on the top deck where there was ample provision of light and air, and with provision for closing the window spaces when necessary. Food and water was stored in bins or containers on the two lower decks. He makes no mention, however, of where the wastes were stored.

119

"Window" Meant "Light"

There have been some misconceptions about the windows of the Ark. From the text of Gen. 6:16, "A window shalt thou make . . ." it would seem the Ark contained only one window. Yet how could one window admit enough light and air to satisfy the needs of the animals and people? Dr. Filby explains it this way:

The word used here for window, TSOHAR, is never again used in this sense in the Old Testament, and it is quite different from the word CHALLON used in Genesis 8:6 where Noah opened "the window which he had made" to release the birds. It is also different from the word ARUBBAH used in Genesis 7:11 for the "windows of heaven."

Obviously this unusual word TSOHAR requires further investigation. Now the word comes from a root meaning to "mount (in the sky) mid-day, or to shine." Its cognates mean "glitter, glisten or shine," and one similar word means "oil" which is used to give light or to make things shine.

But surely conclusive is the fact that on every one of the other 23 occasions in the Old Testament where TSOHAR occurs it means noon, mid-day. The word plainly means light, as of the mid-day sun, and is given by other authorities as "brilliance."

Dean Alford (*Commentary on Genesis*, p. 37) translates the passage "Light shalt thou make for the ark." As there was no glass available in such early times it is obvious that this space was open and would admit air.

Thus God made provision for light and air, two essentials for the living creatures in the Ark. It would seem that the "window" or "light" was an open space running possibly nearly the full length of both sides just below the roof which would doubtless be slightly sloping and overhang by a sufficient amount for the rain to fall clear of the walls. This space or light may have been a cubit in height or possibly the text means that the roof was a cubit above the windows: the meaning of the verse is uncertain.

The "window" would be divided at intervals by the main beams either of the cross-walls or of additional "ribs" used to strengthen the whole structure. The "light" would, in fact, consist of many rectangular windows. These could be closed by sliding wooden panels. . . .

Further those which came opposite any rooms in which birds were housed would require a lighter, open, lattice work to prevent the escape of these creatures and it is for this reason that the writer in Genesis 8:6 uses the other word, which in the Old Testament always means a lattice type window. Such a lattice, as we see from Old Testament references, could be slid aside or opened, just as we are told Noah did, for the release of birds.[12]

We tend to agree with Dr. Filby that the windows for light and air were below the roof rather than adjacent to the catwalk on top of the roof, as stated by Hagopian in his eyewitness account. However, we do believe Hagopian saw numerous holes in the roof near the catwalk but interpreted their significance incorrectly.

We believe the holes which Hagopian saw were created after the Flood in the latter days of Noah's confinement on the Ark, for it says in Genesis 8:13 ". . . Noah then removed the covering of the ark and saw that the surface of the ground was drying up."

Gopherwood White Oak?

The Ark wasn't meant to go anywhere. It had no tiller, no rudder and no oars. Although it was doubtless the world's first ocean going vessel, it simply floated. And float it did—more than 900 miles to reach Mt. Ararat in 150 days, according to most scholars who suspect the Ark was built that far away, on either the Tigris or Euphrates rivers.

God's instructions to Noah were to make the Ark of

121

"gopherwood." To this day no one knows exactly what gopherwood is—or was. We can only speculate.

The usual suggestions by scholars are cypress or cedar. But both of these trees are mentioned elsewhere in the Bible with their ordinary Hebrew names. Still others have suggested that gopherwood is oleander.

Proponents of cypress say that the ancient Phoenicians used cypress for shipbuilding because of its lightness and durability. Others say the Egyptians found cedar to be the best wood for making large boats in dynastic times. Oleander, related to the olive tree, can easily be ruled out because it's too bushy and not suitable for producing sturdy planks or beams.

More contemporary scientists are suggesting that gopherwood might have been white oak—at least for the structural beams, with cypress or cedar for planking.

White oak was widely used for shipbuilding, particullarly in the Orient for the construction of wooden naval ships. Today, it is still used in the construction of mine sweepers.

Richard Bliss, adjunct professor of science at the University of Wisconsin, thinks the Ark was made of white oak. During a March, 1976 interview he offers several good reasons why:

It is found growing abundantly in the peri-Mediterranean region and it was probably the "poor man's wood". It was most likely free—all Noah had to do was cut it and take it. Other types of wood would have had to be "imported" from outlying areas, involving an expense to Noah.

White oak is virtually an indestructible wood. It's highly waterproof and retains its natural moisture well because of its unique cellular structure. It's a hard, compact, high density wood and is very suitable for shipbuilding. The wood can be hard to work, but it always splits clean.

Then too we have to keep in mind that most scholars believe Noah spent upwards of 100 years building the Ark.

If he had used another kind of wood such as red oak, the first planks and beams that he put on would have dried out or decayed before he finished the Ark years later. Basically the same decomposition process would have occurred with cypress. But white oak as it drys becomes more compact and experiences a density gain making it more waterproof and highly desirable for any building project spread over a long duration of time.

Pitch Plentiful

Whatever it was made of, we know the Ark was made waterproof. Noah was commanded to "cover it inside and out with pitch."

The word translated as "pitch," says Dr. Filby, also means bitumen, a mineral pitch or asphalt used to seal joints and cracks against water and moisture.

The bituminous substance is found in the oil-bearing regions around the ancient crescent from the Dead Sea to Persia. In Roman times, great lumps of it floated on the Dead Sea. Ideal for making ships waterproof, it was found in ample quantity in Babylonia.

"Large amounts came from Hit or Id, a place only ninety miles from Baghdad, and hence probably near to the place where Noah constructed the Ark," says Dr. Filby.

"Certainly Noah would have had no difficulty in obtaining adequate supplies for the Ark. In shipbuilding it was 'filled' or reinforced with chopped straw, rushes or reeds, sometimes up to 15 percent."[13]

The pitch used by Noah for the Ark was the same used to seal the ark in which Moses was hidden and set afloat on the Nile (Ex. 2:3).[14]

Pitch was widely used in Ziggurat construction, as in the Tower of Babel in Babylonia and in constructional decoration to hold tesserae of limestone, as such recovered architectural embellishments attest.[15]

The Ark was made waterproof, then, by materials easily available in large quantities in the very area where it most likely was built.

Did the Ark have anchors?

It is assumed that it did, since it was customary for ancient boats to have anchors.[16]

In the late 1930's, "Believe It Or Not" columnist Robert Ripley found what are believed to be the anchors of Noah's Ark in the holy city of Kairouan in Tunisia, North Africa.

Mohammedan legend says Noah used the anchors in tying his Ark to Mt. Ararat. The anchors are so overwhelmingly large that Ripley, posing for a picture beside them, is practically dwarfed by the metal relics. No one has yet been able to refute his claim or offer any alternative explanation for the anchors.

But whether the Ark actually had—or needed—anchors is open to some conjecture since the Bible doesn't specifically mention them.

Who Crewed For Noah?

How long it took to build the Ark is another mystery. Bible scholars seem to agree that it took 120 years, citing Gen. 6:3—"And the Lord said, My spirit shall not always strive with man, for that he also is flesh: yet his days shall be an hundred and twenty years."

The implication is that God gave mankind 120 years to repent before He would destroy the Earth by flood, during which time Noah was to build an Ark.

We do know that God told Noah to build the Ark *after* He had decided to judge the world. But *how long* afterward is not mentioned. Noah was 500 years old before the first of his three sons—Shem, Ham and Japheth—were born. He was 600 years, two months and 17 days old when the flood began. We don't know whether God warned Noah after his sons were born, or before at the beginning of the 120-year reprieve.

It would seem logical that God would tell Noah—the only man on Earth who found grace in His sight—immediately so he would have the full 120 years to warn mankind and build the Ark. If so, the warning would have come before the birth of Noah's sons.

Who, then, helped Noah build the Ark?

Assuming Noah's sons were born one after the other, Shem, presumably the first son, was born when Noah was 503 (Gen. 11:10) and he would have been about 505 when the last one was born. And it would have been several years before any of the sons could do the least amount of work on the Ark.

With enough help, however, Noah could have built the Ark in perhaps as short a time as 25 years. We know, for example, from Egyptian records, that the Great Pyramid was built in 30 years using 100,000 workers. Surely the task of building an Ark about half the size of the *Queen Mary*—assuming Noah had work crews to help him— could be accomplished in less than 120 years.

However long it took him, there is too little evidence in the Bible to support the belief that Noah took from 100 years to 120 years to build the Ark. The only evidence in support of this view is that the flood came approximately 100 years after the birth of Shem, Ham and Japheth.

We are correct in assuming it took many years to build the Ark. But how many is "many years?" Twenty, 30, 40, 100, 120? A lot would depend on how many helpers Noah had.

It doesn't take too much imagination to see that Noah's contemporaries would consider him eccentric—he probably was the laughing stock of the Mesopotamian Valley. But men will work at any job—given the right pay—even if the boss is a bit odd. It would be inconceivable of God to have given Noah a job to build such an Ark without providing him with the resources. It is probable then, that Noah hired crews to cut the timber and help build the ship.

"I think anyone who tries to visualize the construction by four men of a vessel 450 feet long will realize that the size of timbers alone for a building 45 feet high (analogous to a four story apartment building) would seem by their sheer massiveness to be beyond the powers of four men to handle," says Dr. Arthur Custance.[17] Especially when we consider the fact that a good many of those building years Noah's sons were children.

The Bible doesn't say Noah and his sons had to build the Ark without the help of hired men. The Biblical account leaves several questions unanswered. How did Noah finance such a project? How many men did he hire? Did he have trouble getting men? How many years did it take to recruit workers? How many quit because they couldn't take the ridicule? What about sabotage and delays? We can only speculate!

Footnotes
Chapter 8

1. Filby, Frederick A., *The Flood Reconsidered* (Zondervan Corp., Grand Rapids, MI, 1971) p. 80.
2. Huyghe, René, *Encyclopedia of Prehistoric Art*, (1957), p. 62, Fig. 72.
3. Petrie, W. M. Flinders, *A History of Egypt*, (1903 edition), Vol. 1, p. 34.
4. Landström, Björn, *The Ship*, (1961).
5. Lucas, *Ancient Egyptian Materials*, p. 513.
6. Filby, *op. cit.*, p. 100.
7. *Ibid.*, p. 93.
8. *Ibid.*
9. Whitcomb, John C. Jr. and Morris, Henry M., *The Genesis Flood* (Presbyterian and Reformed Publishing Co., Nutley, N.J. 1961) p. 11.
10. Filby, *op. cit.*, p. 88.
11. Howe, George F. ed., *Speak to the Earth* (Presbyterian and Reformed Publishing Co., Nutley, N.J., 1975), pp. 294-299.
12. Filby, *op. cit.*, pp. 94-96.
13. *Ibid.*, p. 97.
14. Nave, Orville J., *Nave's Topical Bible* (Moody Press, Chicago, IL, 1974) reference "Pitch".
15. Unger, Merrill F., *Unger's Bible Dictionary* (Moody Press, Chicago, IL, ed. 1974 c. 1957) reference "Pitch".
16. Freeman, Rev. James M., *Manners and Customs of the Bible* (Logos International, Plainfield, N.J., 1972), p. 454.
17. Custance, Arthur C., *The Extent of the Flood: Doorway Papers #41* (published by the author, Ottawa, 1958), pp. 8-9.

127

CHAPTER 9

The Flood Survivors Aboard the Ark

Probably nothing about the Ark account causes more curiosity than the animals and the people themselves.

How was it possible to gather representatives of every type of animal? How many different kinds of animals were aboard? What was the total number?

How did Noah, his wife, his sons and their families live? How could eight people care for the animals? What happened to them after the Flood? And how did the Flood affect their life span?

These are all valid questions. And again we can turn to scientists and Bible scholars for the answers.

Biblical historians say that gathering the animals was not difficult.

The Lord commanded Noah to "cause the animals to come into the Ark." *Noah was not told to gather representative creatures of every kind.* He was told that the animals would come to him—no need for elaborate trapping expeditions.

Animals used their God-given instincts to guide them to the Ark.[1] In Gen. 7:15-16, it says, *"the coming ones* came male and female of all flesh." Note also Gen. 6:20 in which God said the animals *"shall come to you to be kept alive"* (New English Bible). These passages indicate that the animals came to the Ark of their own accord. This is a perfectly believable explanation. Birds and animals are known to do incredible things by instinct.

Clean and Unclean

Dr. Arthur J. Jones, a scientist at Bournville College in Birmingham, England, has done years of research on the kinds of animals and the number that went aboard the Ark. Much of his research is based on a thorough analysis of the original usage of Hebrew terms.

In a recent series of scientific articles published in America, Dr. Jones explains that representatives of all the major groups of animals were taken into the Ark except water swarmers—commonly known as water-dwelling animal groups.

He says all the animals taken into the Ark are described as *basar*, meaning flesh animals with blood; thus only the following groups were taken aboard:

1. All birds.
2. All land-dwelling reptiles and mammals.
3. Possibly some of the more terrestrial amphibia.

Noah, he says, was not required to take invertebrates, insects and fish aboard.

Animals were classified as clean and unclean. While it is difficult to know which groups were regarded as clean, Biblical references to animals legally used for sacrifice and/or (in the post-Flood era) for food by the Israelites give us a clue.

Essentially, clean animals were non-flesh eating, chewed a cud and had a divided hoof. Also many non-predatory birds were considered clean, while camels (chew the cud, but do not have divided hoof) and pigs (have divided hoof, but do not chew the cud) were labeled unclean. A sampling of these clean representatives aboard the Ark would include deer, giraffe, cattle, antelope, sheep, gazelle, goats, pigeons, dodos, sandgrouse, guineafowl, turkeys, song birds, ducks, geese and swans.

The unclean animals were usually those that ate flesh, did not chew a cud nor have a divided hoof. Animals which fell into this group were predatory and scavenging land birds, most water birds, bats, small rodents, lizards, and predatory mammals.

God's first instruction to Noah was that he bring the animals into the Ark in pairs. Later, Noah was told the number of pairs. There would be one pair—male and female—of the unclean animals, but seven pairs of the clean animals—male and female, or 14 animals in each clean group.

Bible students disagree on this point. Some contend there were only seven of each clean group, or three pairs plus one which Noah would sacrifice after the Flood.

Dr. Jones, however, argues the seven-pair theory.

"Four times (Gen. 6:19-20; 7:2-3, 8-9, 15) the account emphasizes that all the animals were taken into the Ark in pairs," he says. "The account also makes it clear that the purpose was propagation: 'to keep seed alive upon the face of all the earth' (Gen. 7:3).

"The reasons for taking seven times more clean animals than unclean seems straightforward: first, clean animals were required for sacrifice; second, they would be required to provide clothing and food (cf. Gen. 9:3) after the Flood (the environment being radically changed); third, as these were becoming vulnerable prey animals they required a head start for survival (cf. Gen. 7:3)."[2]

Besides bringing the animals into the Ark in pairs, God instructed Noah to choose clean and unclean animals and birds "after their kind" (Gen. 6:20).

Dr. Jones says that the Biblical *kind* is "generally equivalent to the *family* of our current vertebrate classifications, although the separate created kinds may have been much smaller in scope than the families of modern taxonomy."[3]

Scientists, including Dr. Jones, place the number of kinds of animals aboard the Ark at between 628 and 800, putting the total number of clean animal kinds at between 24 and 66 and the unclean between 604 and 734.

Dr. Jones explains how these kinds are proportioned in numbers aboard the Ark:

At one pair for each unclean kind and seven pairs for each clean kind, this gives extreme estimates of 1,544 and 2,392 for the number of animals taken into the Ark.[4]

Dr. Jones prefers the lower estimate.

While the number of clean animal kinds is significantly

130

less than the unclean, note that each clean kind is multiplied by 14 (seven pairs), and each unclean kind is multiplied by two. While the ratio of unclean kinds to clean is greater, the number of clean animals and birds is 12 times that of the unclean.

Scientists have pointed out the correlation between the greater number of clean animals taken into the Ark and their present diversity, as compared to the single pair of unclean animals and their present exiguity.[5]

How Animals Survived

How did the animals get along on the Ark? It is reasonable to assume that any hostilities ceased. According to the prophecy of Isaiah 11:6-7, it's possible.

The wolf also shall dwell with the lamb, and the leopard shall lie down with the kid; and the calf and the young lion and the fatling together, and a little child shall lead them.

And the cow and the bear shall feed; their young ones shall lie down together: and the lion shall eat straw like the ox.

Yet when they disembarked and scattered after the Flood, the restraint was lifted, and they returned to their basic natures. The Ark didn't alter their dispositions, but God had kept them peaceable during their long confinement.[6]

Many scientists and scholars have offered theories on how Noah's family cared for the animals. Some have pointed out that with about 2,000 animals aboard, it would mean that during a 12-hour day each member of Noah's family would have had to feed one animal every three minutes.

Dr. Jones, however, dismisses such calculations as meaningless.

"If some university or zoo staff members were to so meditate on the number of animals in their charge, they would soon look for another job," he says.

131

"Noah and his family would certainly have a lot to do, but it does not take that long to look after animals."[7]

Dr. John C. Whitcomb, Jr., and Dr. Henry Morris, in their book *The Genesis Flood*, suggest hibernation as a possible solution to extensive care.[8] Dr. Frederick A. Filby argues against hibernation on the grounds that God would not command Noah to bring food aboard for hibernating animals.[9]

Whitcomb and Morris do not suggest the animals slept throughout the Flood year; the hibernation theory allows animals to sleep during the worst periods. The conditions aboard the Ark—falling temperature, reduced light, restriction on movement—were conducive to sleep for many animals.[10]

Occasional short periods of unfavorable conditions will prompt many animals to sleep; and large animals, such as bears, will stay semi-dormant in their dens for months during the winter. In the tropics, many small animals go to sleep to avoid the peak of the dry season, a phenomenon called aestivation.

Animals don't remain in hibernation indefinitely. They arouse periodically—rhythmically every few days or weeks—then go back to hibernation.[11]

"As soon as conditions on the Ark improved the animals probably awoke and ate," Dr. Jones says. "The ability to enter into prolonged 'sleep' is probably a common property of animals." That property was originally intended very possibly to meet the need for a period of rest.[12]

It also is a widespread mechanism in the animal kingdom for surviving periods of climatic adversity.

"Practically all reptiles and amphibians have the capacity of hibernation," says Dr. Morris. "Mammals, being warm-blooded, do not have as great a need for it, and so at present, relatively few practice it. Nevertheless, it is probable that the latent ability to do so is present in practically all mammals."[13]

Many invertebrates hibernate for long periods. And it is known that at least one bird, the *poor-will*, hibernates. The hummingbird also exhibits nightly many of the characteristics of hibernation.[14] Fundamentally, birds do possess latent capacity to hibernate.

Whitcomb and Morris suggest birds don't need to hibernate because their power of flight makes long migrations a more effective means for coping with bad weather and other adverse conditions.[15]

It is logical to conclude that during the Flood, the remarkable abilities of animals to adapt to adverse conditions were intensified. Whitcomb and Morris comment further on this:

> It seems rather likely that climatic conditions before the Flood were so equable that these particular abilities were not needed then. Perhaps it is significant that, after the Flood, God's pronouncement that "cold and heat, and summer and winter" (Gen. 8:22) would henceforth come in regular cycles is immediately followed by statements concerning the animals that seem to imply changes in animal natures and relationships to mankind (Gen. 9:2-5).
>
> Even as God instructed Noah, by specific revelation, concerning the coming Flood and his means of escape from it, so He instructed certain of the animals, through impartation of a migratory directional instinct which would afterward be inherited in greater or lesser degree by their descendants, to flee from their native habitats to the place of safety.
>
> Then, having entered the Ark, they also received from God the power to become more or less dormant, in various ways, in order to be able to survive the year in which they were to be confined within the Ark while the great storms and convulsions raged outside.[16]

While the Bible is silent on this explanation, it is nevertheless a plausible one. And one which defies a better theory. It would thus not be a difficult task for Noah and his family to care for the animals.

Animal care involved more than feeding, of course. Stalls and cages would have had to be cleaned daily—at least when the animals were not hibernating. Manure would most likely have been stored on the lower deck. Computations by some San Diego zoologists indicate that up to 800 tons of manure accumulated in the lower deck during the year aboard the Ark.

How Noah and his family lived in the Ark also is intriguing.

The Bible says there were only eight persons aboard—Noah and his wife; his sons, Shem, Ham and Japheth and their wives. However, Noah was about 500 years old when his sons were born. In all probability, Noah and his wife had many children during the first 500 years of his life. Shem, Ham and Japheth are mentioned because of their significance to the Biblical record.[17]

What happened to the rest of Noah's family, the Bible doesn't say. They could have been wicked like their contemporaries and died in the Flood; or they could have died of accidental causes before the Flood.

Noah Family Probably Comfortable

We can only speculate, too, on Noah's living conditions aboard the Ark. But living space and food requirements for four couples for a year would have been substantial. We have already noted the size of the Ark, that it had a volumetric capacity equal to that of 569 standard railroad stock cars. It is estimated that the Ark could have carried more than 100,000 animals of the size of sheep. However, the Ark was not built to transport stock, but for long-term living conditions that would require a large amount of space.

Room would have been ample for food and water storage, sanitation storage, and exercise of the animals, with sufficient internal free space to prevent unbearable fouling or heating of the air. Possible reproduction during the year by the animals would require more space. So the Ark was built to maintain the best possible conditions for life.

With such provision for the animals, it is logical to assume the eight persons aboard also were comfortable. We must not ignore, either, the woman's touch to the living quarters. We can assume Noah's wife and daughters-in-law made their cabins as pleasant as possible under the circumstances.

What kind of beds did they sleep in?

A bed in Biblical days was simply a mat or blanket that could be carried in the hands. Wealthy people had quilts or mattresses filled with cotton, which they spread on the floor or on a divan. The poor often had no bed, except their outer garment. We can hardly consider Noah poor; he would have had to have wealth to hire work crews for the Ark.

It is possible that divans were built in the family's living quarters. Divans were a platform about three to four feet wide. Sometimes in Biblical days they extended across one end of the room or around three sides and were elevated from six inches to a foot above the floor. By day, they were used as a sofa; by night for sleeping.[18]

Noah's family probably had other furniture, even tables for eating. Modern Arabs usually have nothing but a piece of skin or leather, a mat, or a linen cloth spread upon the ground for a table. Ancient Hebrews are supposed to have used a similar "table." But the ancient Egyptian table was a round tray fixed on a stone or hardwood pillar or leg.[19]

We don't know, of course, what the living customs were during pre-Flood times, but can assume that furnishings after the Flood evolved from the craftsmanship, designs and traditions of Flood survivors.

Vegetarian Diet For All

What did the people on the Ark eat?

Noah was commanded to bring food aboard the Ark for both the animals and his family.

Gen. 9:2-3 implies that before the Flood, people were vegetarians. After the Flood, God put the fear of man in the animal kingdom and told Noah, "Every moving thing that liveth shall be meat for you; *even as the green herb* have I given you all things." Meat became part of the post-Flood diet. The phrase "even as the green herb"

135

strengthens the evidence that Noah and his family were vegetarians before and during the Flood.

We can assume their diet included milk, eggs, bread, nuts, fig cakes, raisins, cheese, grains, grapes, herbs, olives, wheat, and other similar foods since all these existed in ancient Biblical times.

To make bread, Noah's family would have needed some means for baking. One type of oven still used in the Middle East today is a great stone pitcher. A fire is made in the bottom among small flints that retain the heat. The dough is placed on these flints and is soon baked. Sometimes the dough is rolled out very thin and stuck on the outside surface of the heated pitcher. When it's baked, it falls off. Perhaps such an oven existed in Noah's day.

There is a reference to a frying pan in Old Testament times (Lev. 7:9). It was a deep vessel of iron used for boiling meat and could also be used for baking bread. Also, there is the pan, a thin, flat iron plate on which bread could be quickly baked as on the griddles we have today.[20] It is conceivable that baked foods were part of Noah's diet.

Other cooking and eating utensils could have included earthenware pots and bottles, and skins.[21] These were common in Biblical days. We also know from the Bible that pre-Flood craftsmen were skilled in metal works. It is conceivable that some of Noah's utensils were made of copper, gold or silver. They could have been quite fancy.

How Calendar Was Kept

Noah and his cargo were aboard the Ark for about one year and 10 days. In early times, calendar months had no names; they were simply numbered.[22] And so it was in Noah's time. Noah probably kept his calendar by marking the days on the wall of the Ark. The Babylonian Gilgamesh Flood account (10th Tablet, lines 209-212) mentions marking the days on the wall.

According to the old calendar in use during Noah's time, the Flood began on the 17th day of the second month of Noah's 600th year, later known as Marcheswan.

This month ran from a date in October to one in November. Since Noah's months usually began in the middle of one of our months, the Flood must have started early in November. When the waters had receded and Noah left the Ark, it was the 27th day of the second month of the following year. The old world perished in November, and a new era began a year later in the same month.[23]

The destruction and commencement of the world in the month of November is enshrined in the memory of the human race. To many people around the world, November brings the Day of the Dead. In many ancient and contemporary primitive calendars, November also brings a New Year at a time which has neither solstice nor equinox nor astronomical event to justify it.

Many Still Observe Day of Dead

Dr. Filby, in his book *The Flood Reconsidered* (p. 107-108), explains the widespread recognition of the Day of the Dead:

November 2 is all Souls' Day—the Day of the Dead. In France it is Le Jour des Morts—christianized now for centuries but still at heart the Old Day of the Dead when flowers are taken to the tombs. From South America to Northern Europe, from Mexico to Polynesia gifts and flowers are placed on tombs on this anniversary of the Day of Death.

The Persians commenced their New Year in November in a month which was named Mordad-month meaning of the angel of death. In Peru the New Year commenced in November. Mexicans, too, kept the Day of the Dead at the same time of the year.

Natives in parts of Australia at this time of the year paint white stripes on their legs and arms and ribs to resemble skeletons. Our Anglo-Saxon ancestors called November Blood-month! The Celtic inhabitants of England—whose traditions incidentally are among the most ancient in the world—kept their New Year in November.

The ritual has in some cases been absorbed into, or modified by, later religions but the recollection of that Day of Judgment and Death has never ceased.

The Flood began and ended in November, lasting little over a year—but the recollection of it has never died out in the memory and the calendars of the descendants of that little group of survivors.

Let's review the sequence of events in the Flood period:

It rained 40 days and nights after the Flood began, or until the 26th day of the third month, November-December by modern equivalent. The Ark rested upon the waters another 110 days for a total of 150 days, coming to rest on a slope of Mt. Ararat on the 17th day of the seventh month or March-April. The tops of the mountains were seen in June-July, the first day of the 10th month. About July-August—40 days to the 10th day of the 11th month—Noah released the birds.

Noah judged that the waters had dried up by the first day of the first month of his year 601, or about September-October. About 56 days later—the 27th day of the second month of Noah's 601st year—Noah left the Ark, 370 days after the Flood began.[24]

The 370-day period assumes a lunar calendar month of 30 days. Some scholars put the stay aboard the Ark at 375 days, figuring 365 days a year plus 10 days.[25]

It was natural for Noah to send out a raven and a dove to determine if the flood waters had subsided. In ancient times animals were often used for communication and navigational purposes. Doves or pigeons, with their powerful homing instincts, have always been famous for their ability to undertake long, swift flights. To assume that Noah knew this is more than reasonable.

Pigeons were used as messengers in the days of Solomon.[26] The Romans used them during battles, and the Greeks used them to carry the results of the Olympic games. Many amazing flights were made by these birds in World Wars I and II. Through mist and storm and shrapnel, literally hundreds of pigeons carried their messages that saved the lives of thousands of wrecked airmen and troops cut off by enemy forces.

What Olive Leaf Showed

Greek tradition has that the first olive branch to reach Greece was brought by a dove from Phoenicia. Olive groves are favorite places for doves to build their nests. No wonder Noah's dove returned to the Ark with "a freshly plucked olive leaf."

Noah apparently knew the habits of animals, and he knew that the raven—a scavenger bird—would not return to the Ark if the water had subsided enough for it to perch on some slimy surface or carcass. And this is exactly what happened.

The dove is a clean bird; it would not perch on a carcass or slimy surface. Noah sent it out three times. The second time, the dove returned with an olive leaf in its mouth. This told Noah that the Earth was returning to its fruitfulness.

While an olive tree may grow in water, it doesn't grow at mountaintop heights and as a rule prefers slopes below 3,000 feet. Thus, Noah knew that the lower elevations were beginning to produce vegetation.

Whitcomb and Morris say, before it was discovered by the dove, the olive leaf would have had as much as four months to sprout from an asexually propagated olive branch buried near the surface of the soil after exposure to sunshine.[27]

The olive, one of the hardiest of all plants, would be one of the first to sprout after the Flood. Full-grown olive trees can survive extremely harsh treatment. That the dove brought back an *olive* leaf is significant.

Only a few months are needed from the time of implantation of olive cuttings until the leaves sprout. Branches of olive trees apparently were buried near enough to the surface of the soil to sprout shoots, thus

139

producing a new generation of trees from asexually propagated plants, says Dr. Walter Lammerts, a California horticulturist.

The record of the olive leaf and the dove harmonizes with what is known of the nature of the olive tree and with the Bible account of the Flood.

Seven days after the dove returned with the olive leaf, Noah sent it out again. This time the bird didn't return, an indication that the waters had almost completely subsided.[28]

About 29 days later, Noah removed part of the Ark's covering to investigate (Gen. 8:13), and saw that the ground was dry. Noah waited another 56 days before disembarking.

Life Span Shortening

It was a different world after the Flood.

As we have shown, the Earth before the Flood was encircled by a water vapor canopy that created a greenhouse effect on the planet. Temperatures were tropical and mild from pole to pole, preventing air-mass circulations and resultant rainfall. The canopy also filtered out harmful radiation from space, reducing the rate of somatic mutations in living cells, which drastically decreased the rate of aging and death.

The Flood, which marks the great division between the original and present worlds, altered the structure of the Earth's atmosphere, hydrosphere, lithosphere and biosphere by a cataclysmic change in the external behavior of the processes of nature.[29]

With Earth's protective canopy gone, destructive forces were loosed. For the first time, man, animals and all of nature were unleashed. For the first time, man, animals, and plant life felt the sting of cold, the ravages of winds and storms; the blistering temperatures of desert and tropical heat. The ravaging Flood and resultant climatic changes left Planet Earth virtually ruined, its vast, once fertile land areas submerged in great oceans or under barren sands driven by hot winds.

To be sure, not all Earth's beauty was destroyed. But it was no longer the paradise of original creation. And nature began to decay at a more rapid rate.

This has affected man's life span and quite possibly his size or height.

Now Span Is Three Score and Ten

Before the Flood, man lived more than 900 years. Adam, for example, lived for 930 years (Gen. 5:5); Enos lived to be 905, Cainan lived to be 910; Jared, the father of Enoch, died at age 962. Methuselah lived the longest of all—969 years. Noah's father, Lemech, died at age 777 (Gen. 5:31). Noah lived to be 950 years, 350 of which were after the Flood (Gen. 9:28-29).

After the Flood, man's life span decreased sharply to "three score and ten." Shem, Noah's first son, lived to be 600. He was about 97 when the Flood began. Shem's son, Arphaxad, lived only 438 years. By the first generation after the Flood, the life span had decreased nearly 500 years.

By Abraham's time, life was considerably shorter. Abraham is described as an "old man, full of years" who died "in a good old age" at 175 years (Gen. 25:8). His wife, Sarah, was 127 years when she died. Isaac lived 180 years, Jacob 147 and Joseph 110. A few hundred years later, King David lived to be only 70, which is the present life span promised by God ("three score and ten"—Psalm 90:10). Even with modern science's war against major diseases and far better nutrition, we haven't been able to advance the average life span beyond God's 70-year limit.

Why Life Shorter

Let's explore some of the reasons for longevity in pre-Flood times and why it decreased after the Deluge.

The declining life span seems to be linked with the dissipation of the Earth's vapor canopy, say Whitcomb and Morris.[30] The most important effect of the canopy was its shielding action against the intense solar radiation bombarding the Earth from space.

The canopy protected life against lethal long wave radiation. Today ozone is concentrated in the ionesphere and fluxes down because of the planetary wind systems.

We breathe in ozone in 2 or 3 parts per 100 million. Ozone is a very toxic gas, which reacts with the hemoglobin and lympids and creates a domino chain reaction among the molecules in the human system.

Ozone experiments have shown that not only do white blood cells rush to the lungs, but all the vital processes of an organism react. And one of the effects of ozone poisoning is aging. Ozone did not flux down before the Flood. Today it does and is a major cause of aging.[31]

On the other hand, we can be thankful for this ozone layer in the upper atmosphere of the Earth, according to the *Encyclopedia of Atmospheric Sciences* (p. 720). This very thin, protective layer—now a major concern of scientists who believe the use of fluorcarbons in aerosol sprays is destroying it—does stop a tremendous amount of lethal solar radiation from reaching the Earth's surface.

Scientists have definitely discovered that overdoses in radiation can contribute to premature aging.

Dr. Shields Warren, a cancer research specialist, concludes, "Both animal experiments and observations of the life spans of radiologists indicate that a dose of 1,000 roentgens received over a long period of time may well shorten the life span about 10 percent.

"Data on the longevity of more than 82,000 physicians indicate that the average length of life of those not known to have had contact with radiation in the period of 1930 through 1954 was 65.7 years as against an average life span of 60.5 years for the radiologists. Not only is leukemia more prevalent among those exposed, but death from causes such as heart disease and arteriosclerosis also appears to come at an earlier age."[32]

Even more significant are the genetic effects of radiation which can not only injure the person exposed, but his descendants as well. Scientists say that radiation is the chief cause of mutation; that is, permanent hereditary changes in the genetic structure of the germ cell.[33]

The pre-Flood canopy blotted out the ultra-violet and cosmic rays which cause aging. With the precipitation of the canopy, however, these rays got through the atmosphere, and the aging process was speeded up.

Studying the decreasing life span after the Flood, we see how such radiation affected the Flood survivors and their descendants.

Before the Flood, the canopy provided a warm, pleasant and healthful environment. Man was shielded from radiation and lived a relatively sheltered life. The ground was fertile; presumably no disease existed.

But the Flood changed that. The post-Flood world was plagued by drastic climatic changes. "The rigors of putting up with season changes would have some toll on life," says Dr. Charles McGowan, a medical doctor in Youngstown, Ohio.

One of the post-Flood changes affecting man's life style was his diet. Before the Deluge, he ate vegetables, fruit and nuts. In Gen. 1:29, God told Adam, "Behold, I have given you every herb bearing seed . . . and every tree, in which is the fruit of a tree yielding seed; to you it shall be for meat."

But after the Flood, man could add meat to his diet. God told Noah, "Every moving thing that liveth shall be meat for you; even as the green herb have I given you all things" (Gen. 9:3).

Dr. McGowan says disease and a high cholesterol count are among the bad effects of eating meat.

Heart disease and high blood pressure can be attributed to the meat diet. Autopsied still-born babies have been known to have cholesterol streaks in their arteries—simply because their mothers ate food containing cholesterol. Certain kinds of meat, he says, carried disease such as rabbit fever and trichinosis. God told the Jews not to eat pork, for example, because of the danger of trichinosis.[34]

Glands No Longer Active

According to Dr. Jacob D. Liedmann, a neurosurgeon living in Israel, the human body is capable of living about 1,000 years if certain glands were to continue functioning. He agrees that increased radiation does play a role in shorter life spans, but believes God discontinued the functions of some human glands after the Flood.[35]

He explains that the pineal gland, located close to the third ventricle of the brain, just below the corpus callosum, has never functioned in modern man. The thymus gland, located in the breast bone area, stops functioning at puberty. A third group of glands, known as the parathyroids, located between the thyroid and thymus glands, undergoes functioning adjustments in puberty that can directly relate to the proper or improper action of other organs.

Dr. Liedmann says the function of the pineal gland is unknown, but is believed to have been connected with the renewal of cell structures. "Even though it doesn't appear to have any function today, its removal or the severing of connective tissue will result in death," Dr. Liedmann says.

Most medical specialists agree that the thymus is a remnant of an organ functional in our ancestors. Dr. Liedmann believes that when it did function, the thymus contributed to man's life span.

"The functioning changes in these three glands are most likely the major reason for our life span's reduction to about 70 years," he says. "The key to life spans like those mentioned in the Bible is within these glands. People who believe victories over disease and better nutrition will result in considerably longer life spans can only hope to add a few years to man's longevity. The expansion of our longevity is controlled by these glands."

The gland changes also may have influenced the shorter height and size of people after the Flood for the Bible says in Genesis 6:4 "the giants were on the earth in those days. . . ."

New archaeological evidence indicates that ancient man was very tall. This fact is confirmed in a recent *Los Ange-*

les Times article (March 29, 1976, p. 9) telling about a find made by Soviet archaeologists.

> Soviet archaeologists have uncovered an *early* Bronze Age [*Authors' note—the Bronze Age is believed to have occurred between 5,000 and 2,900 B.C.*] tomb in the northern Caucasus mountains [*Mt. Ararat is a part of the Caucasus Range and this entire area from the Black Sea to where the Euphrates empties into the Persian Gulf is generally attributed to being the cradle of civilization before and after the Flood.*] containing the body of a man 7 feet 2 inches tall, the official press agency Tass reported Sunday (*March 28, 1976*).

> The tomb, covered with highly polished stone slabs weighing up to a ton, also contained the body of a woman, household articles, gold pendants, beads and thin plates, Tass reported.

At press time for this book, we had insufficient evidence to say the Soviets found a pre-Flood man, but certainly believe the Russian find offers interesting circumstantial evidence which should be investigated further.

After the Flood, God told Noah and his sons to "Be fruitful, and multiply, and replenish the Earth" (Gen. 9:1).

Man's longevity then, and for several hundred years afterward, would have made the population increase rates abnormally high.

Population Then and Now

Men had large families in pre-Flood days, and there is evidence that this practice continued after the Flood. The age of fathers at the birth of each of the *named* sons ranged from about 30 years in the case of some of Shem's descendants to 500 years in Noah's. Longevity declined after the Flood, but for centuries after the Flood, men still lived and procreated for hundreds of years at a time. Due to the combined effect of long lives and large families, mankind rapidly filled the Earth (Gen. 1:28 6:1, 11) before and after the Flood.

Whitcomb and Morris estimate that the Earth's population was as high as one billion at the time of the Flood.[36] Others have estimated it at only a few million.

The table of nations in Genesis 10 and the account of dispersion in Genesis 11 also indicate large early post-Flood population explosions.

The "population explosion" is a topic of much current interest. The average family size today, worldwide, is about 3.6 children, and the annual population growth rate is 2 percent. Growth planners would like to see these figures reduced to 2.1 children and a corresponding growth rate of 0 percent, so that the world population will not increase but remain at its current level.

Whatever problems population increase may or may not pose for the future, the study of man's past to determine how the world could have been repopulated since the Flood is a fascinating one.[37]

If we assume 100 generations have been born since the first pair (corresponding to about 4000 years, with 40 years per generation), then the average family size must have been 2.46.

In other words, an average family size of less than 1 ¼ boys and 1¼ girls will produce a population of 3.5 billion people in only 4000 years.

The average annual percentage growth rate to produce the present world population in 4000 years is calculated to be ½ percent per year. This is only one-fourth the present growth rate.

In any case, the preceding chronological theory fits the facts very well and is quite conservative. There is more than enough room here to allow long periods of time when, because of war or pestilence, the population growth rates were far below the required averages.

Another way to look at this Genesis repopulation and worldwide dispersion is in terms of "population doublings".[38] Ever since the famous studies of Robert Malthus (1766-1834), it has been known that human populations have tended to increase geometrically with time. That is, the world population tends repeatedly to double itself at equal increments of time.

We can make a case for the starting population of one man and one woman to have gone through slightly more than thirty "doublings" to reach our current world population.

The time length for one doubling is uncertain. But the following information provides some reasonable means for estimating it:

At the time of the birth of Christ, there presumably were from 200 to 250 million persons on this planet. Some 700 years later, there was about the same number—say 300 million—a long slow decline in total population having been followed by a compensating increase.

It took roughly 950 more years, namely, until 1650, for this 300 million to double to 600 million. But then it took only 200 years, from 1650 to 1850, for the next doubling up to 1200 million, or 1.2 billion. From 1850 to 1950, in only 100 years, the earth's population doubled again, to about 2.4 billion.[89]

The figures for world population prior to the Middle Ages are only guesses. The 1650 figure is the first one with any degree of validity. So from 1650 to 1950, the population increased from 600 million to 2400 million, representing two doublings in 300 years, or a time length for one doubling of 150 years. The next doubling is expected to occur by 1988, taking only 38 years due to major advances in medicine and sanitation.

All things considered, the period from 1650 to 1850 is one that would be about as typical as any for one doubling. We could split the difference between the previous 150-year figure and this 200-year figure (1650 to 1850) and estimate that the most likely length of each doubling is 175 years. This 175 years multiplied by the 30 doublings, leads us back to about 3300 B.C.—within 300 years of the Flood according to Biblical chronology.[40]

"It could not be maintained that this calculation is completely rigorous but it certainly is reasonable—far more so than to say that the population has been doubling itself since a hypothetical beginning several hundred thousand years ago," says Dr. Morris.[41]

How Animals Dispersed

Although billions of insects and fish perished during the flood action, many species survived. Fish that did not get trapped in the sedimentary deposits being laid down by receding flood waters were able to weather the Flood. Most insects reproduce by eggs and therefore many were easily capable of surviving the Flood. Furthermore, there is strong suggestive evidence that many insects rode out the deluge aboard floating debris atop the flood waters. Finally, it would not be difficult to believe that some varieties of insects made it aboard the Ark as stowaways or as planned passengers even though Noah was not required to include them on his embarkation list. Thus the repopulation of insects and fish throughout the world was no doubt easily accomplished.

Present day animal distributions can be explained on the basis of waves of migrations from the mountains of Ararat after the Flood.[42]

Dr. Frank Lewis Marsh makes these helpful suggestions as to how the migrations went:

The journeys from the mountains of Ararat to their present habitats were made in an intermittent fashion, each generation sending representatives a little farther from the original home. The presence of tapirs today only in South America and the Malayan islands, opposite sides of the Earth, is indicative of the fact that animals migrated in more than one direction. . . .

There is no reason for believing that this distribution of animals was accomplished by any other processes than those employed in distribution today. . . . Increase in number of individuals of any one kind causes a necessity for spreading outward toward the horizon in search of food and homes. . . .[43]

It is quite unnecessary to assume that hundreds or even thousands of years were required for animals to attain their present geographical distribution. There is some evidence available which shows that animals could have reached their present habitats with amazing speed, crossing continents and even large stretches of open sea on their way.

In 1883, the island of Krakatoa was left destroyed by a volcanic eruption. For nearly 25 years practically nothing lived in the remnant of that volcanic island.

"But then the colonists began to arrive—a few mammals in 1908; a number of birds, lizards, and snakes; various mollusks, insects, and earthworms," says Rachel L. Carson, in her famous book, *The Sea Around Us*. "Ninety percent of Krakatoa's new inhabitants, Dutch scientists found, were forms that could have arrived by air."[44]

Professor Paul A. Moody of the University of Vermont explains how large land animals have been able to cross oceans on natural "floating islands":

In times of flood large masses of earth and entwining vegetation including trees, may be torn loose from the banks of rivers and swept out to sea. Sometimes such masses are encountered floating in the ocean out of sight of land, still lush and green, with palms twenty to thirty feet tall. It is entirely probable that land animals may be transported long distances in this manner.[45]

We know little of the migrations of animals in the past. But what we do know shows clearly the possibility of rapid colonization of distant areas, even though oceans had to be crossed in the process.

"It would not have required many centuries to migrate from Asia to South America over the Bering land bridge," Whitcomb and Morris say. "Population pressures, search for new homes, and especially the impelling force of God's command to the animal kingdom (Gen. 8:17) soon filled every part of the habitable Earth with birds, beasts and creeping things."[46]

We can conclude from the Biblical account—and a

variety of scientific evidences—that the pre-Flood race of humanity, except for Noah and his family, were destroyed by water. Sharing in this destruction were all the air-breathing animals of the world, except those aboard the Ark. The waters continued to recede until finally the ground was dry. Man and animals could again repopulate the Earth.

From the survivors of the Flood have descended all the races of man and the varieties of animals now in the world. And today the search is on for the ancient Ark, which preserved life on earth from utter oblivion.

Footnotes
Chapter 9

1. Epp, Theodore H., *The God of Creation* (Back to the Bible Broadcast, Lincoln, NE, 1972) pp. 291-291.
2. Jones, Arthur J., "How Many Animals in the Ark?" *Creation Research Quarterly,* Vol. 10, September 1973, pp. 103-104.
3. *Ibid.,* pp. 103-104.
4. *Ibid.,* p. 106.
5. Lammerts, W. E., "The Galapagos Island Finches," *Creation Research Society Quarterly,* 1966, 3 (1): pp. 73-79.
6. Henry, Matthew and Scott, Thomas, "Genesis 6:13-16," *Logos Commentary on the Holy Bible, Genesis to Esther* (Logos International, Plainfield, N.J.,), p. 25.
7. Jones, *op. cit.,* p. 107.
8. Whitcomb, John C. Jr. and Morris, Henry M., *The Genesis Flood* (Presbyterian and Reformed Publishing Co., Nutley, N.J., 1961), p. 71.
9. Filby, *op. cit.,* pp. 85-86. Also, The Genesis Flood (letter to the editor), *The Witness,* 1970, p. 429.
10. See articles in Mammalian Hibernation III (K. C. Fisher *et al.* editors), Oliver and Boyd, Edinburgh and London, 1967.
11. Pengelley, E. T., 1967, "The Relation of External Conditions to the Onset and Termination of Hibernation and Aestivation," *Mammalian Hibernation III. Ibid.,* pp. 1-29.
12. Marshall, F. H. A. ed., *Emigration, Migration and Nomadism* (W. Heffer and Sons Ltd., Cambridge, England, 1931) Chapter IX, pp. 307-320.
13. Whitcomb and Morris, *op. cit.,* p. 71.
14. Matthews, L. H., "The Hibernation of Mammals," 1955, Report of the Smithsonian Institution, 1956, pp. 410-411.
15. Whitcomb and Morris, *op. cit.,* p. 72.
16. *Ibid.,* pp. 73-74.

17. Epp, *op. cit.*, p. 279.

18. Freeman, James M., *Manners and Customs of the Bible* (Logos International, Plainfield, N.J., 1972), pp. 168, 342.

19. *Ibid.*, pp. 51, 226.

20. *Ibid.*, p. 89.

21. *Ibid.*, pp. 171, 286, 344.

22. Filby, *op. cit.*, p. 104.

23. *Ibid.*, p. 106.

24. *Ibid.*, p. 105.

25. *Ibid.*, p. 106.

26. *Chambers Encyclopedia,* Article "Dove".

27. Whitcomb and Morris, *op. cit.*, p. 8.

28. Epp, Theodore H., "Floodwaters Subside," *Good News Broadcaster,* April 1975, p. 28.

29. Morris, Dr. Henry, *Scientific Creationism* (Creation-Life Publishers, San Diego, CA, 1974) p. 213.

30. Whitcomb and Morris, *op. cit.*, p. 399.

31. Patten, Donald "Cataclysm From Space" filmstrip (American Media, 1971).

32. Warren, Dr. Shields, "Radiation and the Human Body," *Scientific Monthly,* Vol. 84, January 1957, p. 5.

33. Whitcomb and Morris, *op. cit.*, p. 401.

34. McGowan, Dr. Charles, speech given in Niles, Ohio, 1975.

35. Liedmann, Dr. Jacob D., Statements made during a March 1976 interview.

36. Whitcomb and Morris, *op. cit.*, p. 27.

37. Morris, *op. cit.*, pp. 167-168.

38. Whitcomb and Morris, *op. cit.*, pp. 396-397.

39. Warren Weaver, "People, Energy, and Food," *Scientific Monthly,* Vol. 78, June 1954, p. 359.

40. Whitcomb and Morris, *op. cit.*, pp. 398.

41. *Ibid.*

42. *Ibid.*, p. 80.

43. Marsh, Frank L., *Evolution, Creation, and Science* (Review and Herald Pub. Assoc., Washington, D.C., 1947), p. 291.

44. Carson, Rachel L., *The Sea Around Us* (Oxford University Press, New York, 1951), pp. 91-92.

45. Moody, Paul A. *Introduction to Evolution* (Harper and Brothers, New York, 1953), p. 262.

46. Whitcomb and Morris, *op. cit.*, p. 87.

CHAPTER 10

20th Century Expeditions and Sightings

For hundreds of years explorers have climbed Ararat looking for the remains of Noah's Ark.

Some sensational events in the 19th century resulted in the recovery of a piece of wood believed to have been part of the Ark. The 20th century saw the most significant sightings of an *intact* Ark as well as one of the most spectacular of wood recoveries.

We have already mentioned in detail the George Hagopian sightings of 1902 and 1904 and the Vladimir Roskovitsky sighting of 1916 and its follow-up reconnaissance expedition.

In 1932, Los Angeles radio station KFI sent reporter Carveth Wells to the Armenian Monastery of Echmiadzin, Russia. They wanted to verify whether Dr. Parrot in 1829 had actually seen a cross or other relic made from the Ark's wood. Wells described what he saw in a small, heavy, golden casket inlaid with precious stones:

> I opened the last casket, which looked very much like an ordinary ikon from the outside, but on opening the two doors of the casket, instead of finding the usual painting of Jesus or the Holy Family, there was a piece of reddish-colored petrified wood, measuring about twelve inches by nine and about an inch thick. The grain was clearly visible. So this was the piece of wood I had come so far to see. . .[1].

In 1936, New Zealander Hardwicke Knight accidentally discovered rectangular timbers on Mt. Ararat while climbing in the direction of Ahora Gorge. The following

153

account was compiled by John Warwick Montgomery from personal correspondence between Ark researcher Eryl Cummings and Knight:

> Knight was still climbing the next day, and ridge was still succeeding ridge, when he crossed one more snow field. He passed the area around Lake Kop, on the northern side of the mountain, but there were still two more ice fields to cross before he could reach the next ridge.

> The weary climber crossed the first, then skirted below the second. He walked over some soggy timbers at the termination of the second ice field, and climbed half way up the slope of the farther side. Was this some ancient trackway, Knight wondered idly as he passed on?

> Suddenly he paused, then turned back. "Anxious though I was to conserve my strength," says Knight, "I was nonetheless curious, even if my curiosity had been slow to take. I satisfied myself that the soggy mass was indeed timber.

> "It reminded me, when I felt it, of the forest trees said to be prehistoric which are submerged by the sea and appear at low tide at Walberswick on the Suffolk coast of England, or of the timbers of a Spanish galleon that are exposed in a similar way at very low tide on the Welsh coast.

Rectangular Timbers Found

> "All around was the stony rubble that had rolled down the mountainside. Timbers extended in more than one direction; some were parallel and others perpendicular to them. The timbers could have been massive rectangular beams, although all I could see was the tops of them exposed level with the surface of the ground and it was not possible to tell how far they extended under the stones."

At first thought, Knight considered the possibility that he might have stumbled on the remains of a gun carriage from some medieval military campaign. The timbers did not look in the least like fallen logs or trees, he assures us, or he would have ignored them. "Not only were they rectangular in themselves," he explains, "but they formed a framework which was also rectangular."

It was impossible to say if the timbers had been hewn, since there was no texture left upon the surface, which the discoverer described as "soggy and dark," and perhaps nine inches to a foot in width, and only a few feet of them were exposed by the melting of the ice field at its lower end.

"The Biblical description of the Ark is explicit," says Knight. "It was an immense structure made of timbers, and what I had seen was not the whole remains of such a structure, and I have never for a moment thought so. The proportions of the timbers, however, make it seem logical to me to suppose that they are part of a very large and necessarily strong structure. Somewhere in or under the ice higher on the mountain above that place there might be a larger portion of this structure preserved."[2]

During World War II, American aviators flew hundreds of flights over Mt. Ararat, taking off from the Allied bases in Tunisia and going to Russia in a major attempt to keep the Red Army supplied.

Search For Stars and Stripes

Several times during those years, reports surfaced about American, Australian and Russian airmen seeing the Ark locked in the glacial mass below. One of these sightings was reported in a summer 1943 edition of the *Stars and Stripes* Army newspaper.

"Because verification of the *Stars and Stripes* story seemed of major importance, a renewed search for the original article was taken up in 1973" says Cummings. "Every possible source of information was tapped—from university libraries and Army archives to officers who had served in Tunisia during that period of time. But the attempts to ferret out one small item in an Army newspaper some thirty years before proved to be a monumental and disappointing task."[3]

Letters still come to the Cummings home in Farmington, New Mexico, mentioning the missing *Stars and Stripes* article. Violet Cummings relates the following account of a 1973 letter she received:

> The husband of the woman who wrote us had been stationed in Tunisia in 1943, she said, connected with a medical unit that followed the front line. He, too, had seen this same story of the flyers who reported seeing a great ship they believed to be the Ark as they flew over Ararat on the Allied supply route to Erivan.
>
> He clipped the article and sent it home for his wife to read. Some time later this man died. Upon her remarriage his wife had sorted through his old effects and came across the clipping again. Not realizing its potential importance—you guessed it—she had thrown it away. Her son also remembered seeing the story, she said.

There had been many theaters of war, and many confusing editions of the *Stars and Stripes*. No one seems to remember the masthead of the particular issue in which the story had been seen, nor the exact date.

In our research, we had Mrs. Roberta Shearin, a staff researcher at the Army Library in Washington, D.C., review each daily issue of several possible regional editions in which the story could have appeared. Editions, which we selected for a daily microfilm screening by Mrs. Shearin, included the Tunisia edition (from December 1943 to June 1944), the Mediterranean (December 1943-January 1944), the North African (May 1943-May 1944) and the Africa-Middle East-Persian Gulf (April 1943-December 1945).

Mrs. Shearin's thorough search, taking about a month, produced no results. We stopped it since there were nearly 25 other editions in the European war theater which possibly could have run the story.

Still other non-military people told us that they had remembered seeing something about the Ark on theater newsreels during the 1940's. This started another massive search by us to locate any such footage in the archives of numerous newsreel film companies.

The major producers of newsreels in the 40's were Pathé, Fox Movie-Tone, March of Time (Time-Life), Universal and Paramount. A catalog search of millions of feet of film produced no footage of the sighting. The film may exist; the subject could have been catalogued under some news event other than the topic of "Noah's Ark on Mt. Ararat."

Liedmann Testimony

But Dr. Jacob D. Liedmann, while serving as an aviator in World War II, remembers seeing some photos of the Ark on Mt. Ararat taken by a Russian aviator. The following is a composite account from Violet M. Cummings' book, *Noah's Ark: Fact or Fable?* (p. 329-331) and from interviews we conducted with Dr. Liedmann in March 1976:

I was born in Sweden of Orthodox Jewish parents who had migrated from the Russian Ukraine following my grandfather's execution by the Russians. From my parents I learned the Russian language as well as the Hebrew and Aramaic languages. I received my medical degree in Uppsala, Sweden . . . my specialty was in neurosurgery.

I had been studying medicine for approximately five years when I quit my studies and volunteered for the RAF for a six month tour of active duty. I fought against the Germans, and was shot down twice by them and was injured in my back. After my recovery, I went back to medical school and began studying hematology at Heidelberg.

It was on one of my trips there that I became acquainted with a Russian Air Force major in Hamburg. I found we had many things in common: we were both squadron leaders during the last portion of World War II; we had both been flying since early manhood; we both spoke the same Russian dialect; he was born in the Ukraine, and my ancestors came from there. Thus we had many common interests to discuss socially.

Sees Photographs

This Air Force major had been a squadron leader in the Russian Air Force and was in command of a group of three planes which had taken in a number of special missions over Mt. Ararat. The first time I met him in 1947, he showed me three distinct pictures taken of Mt. Ararat in 1938 at approximately the 14,000 foot elevation. These pictures also showed a Russian aircraft with their insignia on the wings. Each of these pictures showed a boat-like structure, which he said was Noah's Ark.

One of those pictures showed the ship protruding out of the ice approximately 80 to 90 feet and it was tilted slightly downwards. In the bottom of that area was a little melted pond or lake. The glacier was shown with the mountain summit in the upper right of that picture and the other pictures were taken at a similar angle.

There were several open holes in the side near the top of the structure. They could have been portholes. On top of the super structure there were several holes or damage. I would rather classify them as damage more than I would as planned holes. But the boat structure itself was not damaged at all.

I met the same man a year later in 1948, also in Hamburg. At that time he showed me another set of pictures and said, "These have been taken since I saw you." He showed me almost a dozen pictures. The Ark was covered up much more than the first time with maybe only 12 or 15 feet of the vessel showing. Some sections could be seen through the glassy clear ice.

He wouldn't give me too much information, because as he pointed out time and again, those photographs were the property of the USSR. I even asked him for a copy of these pictures. Again the answer was negative.

Dr. Liedmann's father also had some photos of the Ark, which he remembers seeing as a small boy, but the doctor does not know what happened to them after his father died in Sweden in the 1960's.

Farmer's Testimony

Another story is from a Kurdish farmer named Reshit, who told his fellow villagers that he had seen the Ark in September 1948. His sighting, reported by Edwin Greenwald of the Associated Press on November 13, 1948, occurred two-thirds of the way up Ararat on its north face—the area where most reliable accounts have consistently located it.

Here are excerpts from the Associated Press story:

There, Reshit said, was the prow of a ship protruding from a canyon down which tons of melting ice and snow had been rushing for more than two months. The prow was almost entirely revealed, but the rest of the object was still covered.

The contour of the earth, Reshit said, indicated the invisible part of the object was shaped like a ship. The prow, he added, was about the size of a house.

Reshit climbed down to it and with his dagger tried to break off a piece of the prow. It was so hard it would not break. It was blackened with age. Reshit insisted it was not a simple rock formation.

"I know a ship when I see one," he said. "This is a ship."

He spread the word among little villages at the base of the mountain, and peasants began climbing up its northern slopes to see the weird thing he had found. Each came back and said it was a ship.

"This is no folklore about the Ark," said Shukru Bey, a 69-year-old farmer who owns large acreage in the area. "And persons who saw Reshit's find came away in great surprise. There are no cameras out in this wild isolated country where Turkey, Russia, and Iran meet, hence no one came away with a picture. The snows have been falling again and perhaps have covered it by now."

Greene Testimony

George Jefferson Greene, an American pipeline and mining engineer working in the Middle East, saw a portion of the Ark exposed on Ararat's northeast face in 1952. He was in a helicopter on a reconnaissance mission for his company when he saw the ship protruding from the ice.

Reaching for his camera, Greene directed the pilot to maneuver the craft as close as possible to the huge structure below.

Closer and closer they edged, while the excited engineer filmed his discovery. Sideways, head on, from nearer than 100 feet, the shutter clicked, while the sun began to lower in the western sky. Greene took what turned out to be six extraordinary photographs.

When the photos were enlarged, the joints and parallel horizontal timber were clearly visible. The photos revealed that the boat was situated on a "fault" on the mountainside; that a high cliff protected it on one side and a sheer drop off on the other side. The glacier in which it was buried had only partly melted away, but about a third of the prow was visible from the air.

After failing to interest American friends in helping to finance an expedition to Ararat to recover the Ark, Greene transferred to a mining operation in British Guyana. There on December 27, 1962—ten years after his discovery on Ararat—he was murdered for his gold. All of his belongings, including the valuable photographs, disappeared.

"Over the years I have had contact by telephone or in person with more than 30 people who have seen the photos," says Eryl Cummings, who has spent thousands of dollars trying to locate these photos all over the world. "And I even met one man who had these photos in his possession for two years. But I got to him too late."

Drake Testimony

Dr. Clifford L. Burdick, a geologist and associate of Ark researcher Eyrl Cummings, had a description of the photographs from Fred Drake, an oil man who had been in contact with Greene in 1954.

Burdick interviewed Drake, whom he found in Arizona.

"I've seen actual photographs of the Ark," Drake said. "I was associated with an oil prospecting crew, staying in a motel in Kanab, Utah, about 1954. I became acquainted with an oil engineer by the name of George Greene, who said he had recently returned from Turkey where he had worked for an oil pipeline company. He had a helicopter at his disposal, and during his flights chanced to circle Mount Ararat near the Eastern border of Turkey.

"He was well equipped with cameras to photograph the terrain and pertinent phenomena. As he circled the north and northeast side of the mountain, Greene was startled to spot a strange anomaly, an object protruding from rock debris on a mountain ledge, with the striking similitude to the prow of a great ship, parallel wooden side planking and all.

"These were six clear photographs, taken from different angles as they flew around the ship. I am sure Mr. Greene would have given me one of the photos, had I asked for one.

"I will admit that I had never been much of a Bible believer, but these pictures sure made a believer out of me!"[5]

He said wooden side planking could be identified in the photographed vessel.

Drake later sent Cummings a drawing depicting the scene he had viewed in one of the Greene photos.[6]

Back to Navarra

In August, 1952, the same year in which Greene took his photos, French industrialist, demolition expert, and explorer Fernand Navarra made the first of his four expeditions up Ararat in search of the Ark. During the descent, he noticed at a distance what could be the Ark or a part of it embedded in ice.

Unable to reach the Ark site during his expedition in 1952, he returned again in 1953 and came within 100 yards of the site before he was forced back by bad weather.

In 1955, Navarra and his son Raphael again returned to Mt. Ararat in hopes of making further discoveries. This time they reached the site and discovered hand-hewn wood at the bottom of a 35 foot crevasse in a glacial ice pack.

In 1969, he led an expedition back to the same site where additional wood was recovered. The complete account of each of Navarra's expeditions will be discussed in the Chapter 11.

Although Navarra is thought to be the only explorer since Sir James Bryce in 1876 to have recovered wood believed to be from Noah's Ark, other expeditions and explorers have been searching the slopes of Ararat practically every summer until about 1974 when the Turkish government called a halt to the expeditions—a topic we'll discuss in Chapter 14.

Other Testimony

Eryl Cummings has been actively involved in the search for Noah's Ark since 1945, the result of reading an article in the Australian edition of *Reader's Digest*.

He probably has the most extensive files on the subject ever compiled, and has spent over $100,000 in research. He states that since 1961, he has had personal knowledge of at least 38 expeditions to Mt. Ararat in search of Noah's Ark. "And that doesn't include the French, Austrian, German, Swedish and British expeditions, which have occurred since 1961 and of which I do not have extensive first-hand knowledge," he says.

Cummings has made 10 trips to Turkey in quest of Noah's Ark, his first in 1966. "During these trips I have been on the mountain 16 times for a total accumulated length of about 70 days," he says.

Late comer, Dr. John Warwick Montgomery, made two expeditions to Mt. Ararat with Cummings and later conducted his own. He climbed on the mountain five times—the first time in 1970 when he scaled Ararat's summit.

John Morris, a field geologist from San Diego associated with the Institute for Creation Research, made his first expedition to the mountain in 1972 and returned again in 1973. On three other occasions, he was unable to acquire climbing permits from the Turkish government.

Representatives from the Holy Ground Changing Center, a religious commune in Frankston, Texas, have made five trips to Turkey, the first expedition in 1973. It's not known for sure how many times they actually made it on to the mountain because local Turkish authorities frequently interfered with their plans.

Currently one of the most inactive groups is the SEARCH Foundation, which received massive international publicity in 1969 after Navarra led them to his 1955 artifact site on Mt. Ararat. Their 1970 expedition, which was widely publicized in the news media, ended in failure in Ankara, Turkey, when government officials revoked their climbing permits for reasons that we'll mention in Chapters 13 and 14.

Since the 1970 setback, the SEARCH group has been rather dormant. Several of the leaders have attached themselves to other groups or dropped out of the search altogether.

Frequently, sincere expedition groups obtain Ararat climbing permits in advance from Turkish government officials, but on arrival in Ankara or at one of the government outposts near Ararat, they discover their permits have been revoked.

Expeditions often have spent thousands of dollars only to be faced with returning to the U.S. in defeat or spending the best part of the climbing season convincing or bribing the authorities to regrant their permits.

Although current expeditions have not recovered any

163

wood from Ararat's slope, nor even come away with any concrete sightings of the Ark, some have come back with telephoto pictures of what looks like a boat and could possibly be the Ark on a ledge of Mt. Ararat.

Photographic Proofs

"The picture we have was actually taken in 1966 by one of us on the Archaeological Research Foundation expedition," says Cummings. "It was one of 2,300 35mm slides taken by expedition members that year. Two years later, when I was looking at these slides, I discovered in one of them an object which looked like it possibly could be the Ark.

"It wasn't until 1974, however, that we were able to definitely orient this picture with the mountain itself and to determine the exact location of the canyon containing this object. At this time I am calling it an unidentified object, and that's what we'll call it until we're able to investigate the area on a furture expedition," concludes Cummings.

"This slide has been analyzed carefully, and there is no question that it is genuine. That is, it isn't the result of retouching, nor the superimposition of one photograph on another. The analysis of the slide makes it plain that whatever the object is in the lower left-hand corner, it is foreign to the material of the mountain," says Dr. Montgomery, who is more outspoken about the characteristics of the 1966 Cummings' slide.

Also the Holy Ground Center contends that it has a similar photo taken in 1974, which not only shows the boat-like object, but "what appears to be gunwale planking arching forward into a ship's bow is readily visible in the photographs."[7]

Most serious Ark researchers question whether the Holy Ground Center photo is genuine. Some critics contend that the photo has been retouched. Of course, the solution to this particular controversy will depend upon literal examination of the location shown in the Holy Ground Center photo.

The 20th century has produced exciting wood finds and Ark sightings. But most of the expeditions have been "foot" efforts by explorers who have had to put up with harassment by local Turkish officials over climbing permits, the climatic conditions, and the treachery of the mountain. Given these obstacles, climber-explorers find it difficult to accomplish much in the way of serious Ark hunting.

In Chapter 13 we'll see how space technology has affected the search for Noah's Ark in the decade of the 70's. We'll discuss the role of American spy planes, mapping satellites, military spy satellites, and the CIA's role in this Biblical mystery. Before we do that, let's discuss Navarra's expeditions and his wood recoveries.

Footnotes
Chapter 10

1. Wells, Carveth, *Kapoot,* 1933, pp. 223-229.

2. Montgomery, John, *The Quest for Noah's Ark,* (Bethany Fellowship, Inc., Minneapolis, MN, 1972), pp. 118-120.

3. Cummings, Violet M., *Noah's Ark: Fable or Fact?* (Family Library, New York, 1973), p. 222.

4. Statements concerning the George Greene account made during an interview with Eryl Cummings in March, 1976.

5. Cummings, Violet M., *Noah's Ark: Fact or Fable?* (Creation-Science Research Center, San Diego, CA, 1972), pp. 216-218.

6. Cummings, Eryl, interview, March 1976.

7. Crotser, Tom, "Object on Ararat Said to be Ark," *The Register,* Santa Ana, CA, Feb. 14, 1975, p. E12. Story released by the Associated Press from Dallas, Texas.

CHAPTER 11

The Fernand Navarra Wood Finds:
1955 and 1969

Fernand Navarra, an authority on Turkish archaeology, is the first man in modern times to discover what is believed to be the remains of Noah's Ark and to bring back the only piece of wood from the Ark that has been sufficiently tested.

Navarra who lives in Bordeaux, France, became interested in the Ark when he was five years old. When he fell in a river, his father fished him out and took him to his mother, who, while she rubbed his back, told him the story of the Ark. He often heard about the Ark as he grew up in the Roman Catholic Church, and his fascination increased.

While doing military service in Syria and Lebanon, he met an Armenian named Alim who had lived near Mt. Ararat. Alim told him stories that his grandfather had related about his search for the Ark on Mt. Ararat. Alim also showed him a tiny piece of wood allegedly from the Ark, which had been in his family for centuries. Seeing this piece of wood confirmed in Navarra's mind that the Ark really existed.[1]

He set his mind on climbing Ararat to find the Ark and bring back proof.

In the succeeding years, Navarra studied everything he could find on the subject. By early 1952—15 years after meeting Alim—he determined to seek it firsthand, according to the account in his book *Noah's Ark: I Touched It*.

His first expedition included a friend, two motion-picture cameramen, and a retired staff officer who had studied at the French Museum of Natural History. Navarra provided the funds.

It was the middle of August before the climbers began their ascent, plagued by mosquitoes, 120 degree temperatures, and thunderstorms. Their first goal was to reach the summit.

They followed their guide along a goat trail, then through névés (fields of snow at head of a glacier), pastures, and rocky terrain. The mosquitoes disappeared at the higher elevations, but clouds, with intermittent showers and hail, up to 13,450 feet, hindered their climb over and around numerous blocks of lava.

They set up camp on a plateau covered with such blocks, but with sufficient open surface for the tents. The tents were just up when a blizzard struck, covering the blue basalt with white.

"The mules had suffered, and so had their packs," Navarra recalls. "Every case had been dented or ripped. Milk, jam, chocolate, and alcohol fuel made a horrible mixture. We succeeded in preparing cocoa, which was not quite what it should have been, but at least was hot. Afterward we went to sleep, listening to the snow-muffled night noises. Next day we hoped to reach our goal."[2]

They were up before dawn. Clouds heavy with snow were gathering and a strong icy wind whipped their faces. The snow that had fallen during the night was wet, and their footprints filled with water that froze immediately.

Their guide, Hazam Calatin, walked in front. The path wound between two névés, and a sharp ridge strewn with boulders.

"Moving forward was difficult. We had to scale the blocks, and the slope was steep. After this chaos, the ridge grew even sharper with rocks on which we cut ourselves when we fell."

By 9 a.m. the men reached 15,400 feet. A half hour later, the altimeter read 15,850 feet. Here they stopped, and Calatin refused to go any further. Navarra tells how he and his team continued the ascent alone:

It was not good at such a height to make prolonged halts. We realized this when we set forth again. Our cooled joints rebelled when we started to move. Breathing was difficult. The rarified air, the lower pressure, made us gasp. We had the feeling that the mountain was defending itself. Just lifting an arm was painful, and throwing a pickaxe forward to catch a block seemed impossible.

We wanted to lie down and sleep and put an end to following these stations of the cross, with frequent falls. Under our feet nothing was solid, neither rocks nor ice. We were not walking, but clawing, our bodies stuck to the ground, trying to adhere to the moving wall.

Bruised, with scum on our lips, we finally reached a terrace of hard ice. We broke off pieces which we sucked, hoping to quench our thirst, but this ice did not melt, and worse yet, it was salty.

A sharp wind kept us awake. Above our heads, a cover of dark clouds gathered; underneath us, a sea of lighter clouds. Between the two, as between two shrouds, we were rowing in a moonlike scene, hallucinating, wondering if we were losing our minds . . . .

The altimeter read 16,934 feet. A few steps more and the team would reach the summit of Noah's mountain.[3]

But the most important part of all was yet to be accomplished. "Now I wanted to find the remains of the Ark . . . to explore the west side of the mountain, the side on which the Echmiadzin monks turned their telescope to show Noah's vessel to travelers," Navarra says.

After returning to Bayazid for fresh supplies, they set out for this new adventure. They took the Ahora trail, and as soon as they reached 3,600 feet, they made their first discovery.

"We were very near the western face," Navarra recalls.

"The cap of Mount Ararat, with the sun behind it, outlined a bright, transparent fringe. All of a sudden, we shouted, 'The Ark!'"

"Two-thirds of the way up the mountain, its bow stood out, black on a background of light-colored rocks," says Navarra. "But, when we came closer, we found that this bow was only a spur of rock, the same one the monks pointed out from their monastery, without ever having climbed up to verify what it was. We had not discovered the real thing, but we had put an end to a legend."

"Black Spot" Found

The climbers continued their ascent. The next day, August 17, Navarra spotted what he had long hoped to see.

It had been a cool summer, and the glacier had scarcely melted. In spite of heavy ice and snow, he discovered an astonishing patch of blackness within the ice. He tells what he saw on August 17, 1952:

I was alone on the cap of ice, which in this place was clear of snow. I felt no fatigue, but a great anxiety. In the sky, an eagle circled, carried by the wind.

I crossed an arm of the glacier and climbed to the top of the moraine. On one side, I could see a mountain of ice lined with crevasses, on the other, sheer wall. At the bottom, I saw a dark mass.

This mass was clearly outlined, its lines straight and curved. The general shape, I thought, resembled that of a ship . . . at least fragments of one.

My mind was perfectly clear, and those who knew me had usually given me credit for having common sense.

At that altitude, in that desert of ice, what could it be? The ruins of a building, church, refuge, or house never mentioned in any account, or tradition, never seen by any of these who came to this place? The wreckage of an airplane? No one ever used beams of that size to build a fuselage.

Those remains, I thought, must be what's left of the Ark. Perhaps this is the flat bottom of the Biblical vessel, the top structures of which must have been scattered.

The structure was really there, but out of reach, and I lacked the necessary equipment to go down to the site. All I could do was to locate it as accurately as possible and rejoin my companions, promising myself that I would come back again.[4]

Navarra left the mountain, disappointed; his life's dream within reach, but powerless to touch it. The expedition had been an alpinist's success, but a failure as far as the discovery of the Noah's Ark was concerned because Navarra brought back neither fragment nor photograph.

Second Expedition

He kept his discovery quiet, not willing to be called a liar.

"I could only keep silent and plan for another trip to the mountain," Navarra recalls, which he did in July 1953.[5]

Accompanied by a Turkish photographer, he found his way fairly easily, climbing to within a hundred yards of the site of the timbers. But boulders, perched precariously above, rolled down at the sound of his voice. Navarra was alone; photographer Alaedin Seker had already stopped his climb.

"I was able to get about twenty yards closer," Navarra recalls, "when suddenly I felt faint. My head felt as if it was caught in a vice and about to burst. I could not coordinate my movements, and could think of only one thing—to go back down!"

He sat down and shut his eyes. For ten minutes he felt numb. He found his companion twenty yards lower, pale, curled up between two rocks, visibly in bad shape. Both exhausted, neither spoke during the three hours of the descent to camp.

Navarra's interest grew into an obsession. Night and day he dreamed of dusty Turkish roads, the glaciers, the moraines of rubbled boulder . . . of extraordinary ways he could pull off a fragment of the Ark and bring it back.

Months went by. In September, 1954, Navarra learned that an American, John Libi, had come within thirty yards of the Ark, and that he planned another expedition in 1955. Navarra made up his mind: he would go again.

The Libi story reinforced his conviction that the glaciers had receded. What had not been possible in 1952 and 1953 might be possible in 1955. If the winter was mild, his chances of reaching the Ark would be better.

Third Expedition

In the summer of 1955 he and his family set out for Ararat, and soon he was climbing the mountain, this time with his 11-year-old son, Raphael. "We hiked on the western front of the volcano, straight toward the summit. Along the gentle slope, the sun had burned the grass. For an hour we climbed steadily, till the heat obliged us to halt."

Later they continued their climb, stopping again at 10 p.m. to set up camp for the night at an altitude of 11,500 feet.

About 4 a.m. the next day, they broke camp and once again started up the mountain, now steeper than ever. The climb was getting dangerous. Big blocks of lava rolled off when they set foot on them. By 3 p.m. father and son had reached the everlasting snowfields, 13,750 high.

But they had climbed too high. The glacier that had been the main landmark was behind them. After roping themselves together for safety, they descended fifty yards. It took them a half hour, shivering in the blowing wind, to reach the edge of the glacier.

Raphael and Navarra crossed the glacier with little difficulty, avoiding the crevasses.

"I recognized the spot where a secondary glacier took shape," Navarra recalls, "the spot where, two years before, I had made my discovery."

It was 4:30 p.m. And Raphael was tired. They set up camp. While Raphael slept, Navarra wondered: would he come so close to the Ark again and fail? He felt an indefinable apprehension, as though seized at the throat by an unearthly hand . . . Navarra let Raphael sleep and left the tent to scout around.

Climbing up a moraine which hung a hundred yards above our camping site, I saw, on my left, a sea of clouds. Eventually it dissolved, revealing a mass of ice, the one I had discovered in 1952. The landscape had changed, for at least one third of the ice had thawed. But this was the spot.

When the mist disappeared, I recognized a wide basin on the other side of the icy mass. In this crater, the glacier's branch ended. The branch, frequently called a stagnant glacier, had receded at least one hundred yards, barely flowing into the area where the remains of the Ark rested. The valley bottom was still covered with mist, and I could not distinguish a thing.

How could it be reached? Only by crawling down the crevassed moraine, as full of holes as a sponge. The stagnant icy mass was caught between two steep rock walls three or four hundred yards high. Opposite, the glacier's branch formed a smooth wall of ice fifty yards high.

After I had studied the problem from all angles, I concluded that the only solution would be to climb up this mountain of crevassed ice and inch down the other side of it to the bottom of the basin.[6]

At 7:30 a.m. the next day, July 5, Navarra and Raphael had arrived at the bottom of the mountain of ice which separated them from the site where the Ark rested.

Looming sixty yards above them, was the mountain of

ice, dangerously fragile with its crevasses and ice-bridges. They had to climb, heavy with ladder, ropes, pickaxes, hatchet, wide-blade knives, crampons and cameras. In some places the ice was a light blue; in others, it resembled transparent lace.

They reached the top of the glacial wall about noon. The other side ended in a sheer wall, and they could not see what lay at its bottom. At the end of a rope, Raphael crept cautiously to the edge and leaned over.

"A little bit more," he called. "More—a bit more—"

Navarra played out a bit more rope.

Son Sees The Boat

"There, I can see now. Yes, the boat is there, Papa. I can see it distinctly."

"I almost fainted with joy," Navarra recalls. "But this was no time to let Raphael go! I gave him the camera, and he took the scene in movies."[7]

Still the problem was to reach the basin bottom. "We had to lower ourselves down a bank about as high as the one we had just climbed. But how? The closer we came to the goal, the more inaccessible it looked.

"While I loaded the camera, Raphael walked away, with the climbing rope still around him. Then he called, 'Come and see. There is a very deep crevasse, and you can see daylight at the bottom.' "

"I walked over, not expecting much. Indeed there was a deep, narrow crevasse, with light at the bottom. Yes, this looked like the way down.

"I uncoiled the ladder and tried it for strength. A few minutes later, I was at the bottom of the crevasse, frozen to my bones because of the humidity. A streamlet of water was running.

"The light Raphael had noticed came from a corridor leading into the crevasse. It opened onto a kind of gently sloping terrace, where I got a glimpse of dark, tangled forms. Those could only be the remains of the structure I had observed from the ridge of the moraine two years before. I promised myself to find them again, and here they were!

"I heard a bellowing noise, but it was only Raphael's voice echoing in the corridor. I hurried back up and told him about my find. He was pleased, but not surprised.

"We took from our sacks tools to cut wood from the Ark. Just then, the snow started falling heavily. Fortunately, a few steps away, there was a little hollow where we took refuge. It was a real ice cave, almost square, five yards deep and two yards high—a perfect shelter for a few minutes."[8]

An hour passed, and still the snow fell. To go out was impossible. Navarra and Raphael were imprisoned. They could not keep on with the search, nor could they return to camp.

Caught By Blizzard

"At three in the afternoon, the sky was almost as dark as night. We could only hope that the whimsical temper of Mount Ararat would change, and the weather would clear up soon," recalls Navarra.

They were forced to spend thirteen hours—the entire night—in the ice cave while a blizzard dumped a foot of snow on the crevasse.

They exercised every half hour until morning, burning cooking tablets to keep warm and to prevent the cameras from freezing.

About 5 a.m. they gathered their equipment, attaching crampons, and headed toward the crevasse through the blanket of fresh snow.

"Once at the edge of the crevasse, I lowered the equipment on a rope. Then I secured the ladder and climbed down," Navarra says.

Passing through the corridor, he found the sloping terrace and began to clear off snow, to uncover the dark strips he had seen the day before.

Soon the strips appeared. "This was the worst disappointment of my life," recalls Navarra. "These shapes were not wood, but frozen moraine dust!"

At Raphael's suggestion, Navarra attacked the ice shell with his pickaxe. He had dug a hole no more than eight inches deep when he hit something. Rock or wood?

"I could feel something hard. When I had dug the hole, I broke through a vaulted ceiling, and cleared off as much icy dust as possible."

The Prize

"There, immersed in water, I saw a black piece of wood! My throat felt tight. I felt like crying and kneeling there to thank God. I checked my tears of happiness to shout to Raphael, 'I've found wood!'"

"Hurry up and come back, I'm cold," Raphael answered.

Navarra tried to pull out the whole beam, but couldn't. "It must have been very long, and perhaps still attached to other parts of the ship's framework. I could only cut along the grain until I split off a piece about five feet long."

It was obviously hand-hewn and surprisingly heavy, its density remarkable after its long stay in water.

He took snapshots and movies, then carried his wooden prize to the foot of the ladder. He attached it to the rope and gave Raphael the joy of hauling it up. Back on the edge of the crevasse, Navarra took movies of Raphael hoisting up this ancient piece of wreckage.[9]

It was 7 a.m., July 6, 1955.

"It's hard to describe how you feel at such a moment," Navarra said later.[10] "Suddenly you don't feel the cold; you're not hungry anymore, you feel exhilarated, and you're on a cloud."

He was sure the wood was from the Ark. "There was never any doubt in my mind. I had done so much research and had so many documents that proved that it could only be the Ark."

He had to cut the wood into pieces to keep the weight of it across his knapsack from making him lose his balance on their descent. "I regretted having to cut up such a venerable relic, but felt better about it later on when I split it up in still smaller pieces to submit to various experts."

While most Ark scholars concede that in 1955 Navarra probably found wood from the Ark, they disagree over the Ark's location.

Navarra found the wood slightly under 13,000 feet on the northwest side of Mt. Ararat. Based on earlier eyewitness accounts, the intact Ark had been thought to rest at about 14,000 feet.

Many Ark scholars theorize that the Ark could have been broken or shattered during an earthquake. The main part of the vessel resting at over 14,000 feet, the broken fragments found by Navarra scattered below. But they wanted to be sure.

For that reason the search for Noah's Ark has continued.

Fourth Expedition

Then, in 1969, the famous French explorer agreed to join the Scientific Exploration and Archaeological Research team known as SEARCH.

Navarra would prove for the first time since 1955, that he could lead an expedition back to the same glacial ice pack on Ararat . . . and hopefully, recover more wood.

After retracing his way up the treacherous mountain, the SEARCH team struggled to locate wood in the same crevasses where Navarra had found it. But the crevasses were not melted as deep as they were in '55. No wood could be found in them.

Navarra then decided to probe the bottom of a small pond adjacent to the ice pack. Since the team's probing poles would not reach to the bottom, he began to probe a small run-off stream from the pond.

At 11:15 a.m. on July 31, 1969, Navarra and the SEARCH team struck pay dirt—five pieces of wood resembling planking, the longest piece nearly 17 inches.

This new find confirmed Navarra's discovery . . . and for many scientists all over the world, provided evidence that Noah had indeed stepped forth upon dry land here.

The 1969 discovery also supplied new evidence for the "broken Ark" theory. Scientists have determined that the Navarra Ark fragments were in a nearly stagmant ice pack of the lower part of the Parrot Glacier. This ice pack, moving at least a meter per year, is continually hauling fragments to lower elevations.

It's highly probable that the Ark, once intact at the 14,-000 foot level on the northwestern side of the mountain, broke in half or into smaller fragments due to an earthquake or avalanche, slid down the nearly 1,200 feet, leaving wooden planks and beams to be absorbed into the lower elevation ice flows.

Probably the front of the Ark remains intact, wedged in rocks and ice far above.

This would explain why, at times, the Ark looks as though it protrudes from the ice intact, and why Navarra was able to find pieces of wood from the Ark at about the 13,000 foot level.

The only other wooden beams or planks recovered or observed in recorded times by Sir James Bryce and Hardwicke Knight were also at about this elevation.

What Navarra had taken from the glacial vise of Mt. Ararat was a five foot hand-hewn and squared piece of timber.

Yes, Navarra had found wood. But was it really a piece from Noah's Ark? Navarra believed it was. But he wanted to be sure. He wanted to know the age of the wood, the type of wood, its geographical origin. He decided to have the wood analyzed by leading institutions around the world. The findings, which produced both believers and critics, are discussed in the next chapter.

Footnotes
Chapter 11

1. Navarra, Fernand, interview with Robert Guenette of Sun Classic Pictures, February 9, 1976.
2. Navarra, Fernand, *Noah's Ark: I Touched It* (Logos International, Plainfield, N.J., 1974), pp. 31-32ff.
3. *Ibid.*, pp. 35-36.
4. *Ibid.*, pp. 36-37.
5. *Ibid.*, p. 38.
6. *Ibid.*, pp. 52-53.
7. *Ibid.*, pp. 57-58.
8. *Ibid.*, pp. 58-59.
9. *Ibid.*, pp. 61-62.
10. Navarra Interview, *op. cit.*

CHAPTER 12

An Analysis of the Navarra Wood

Navarra's wood discovery created excitement in certain circles of the scientific community and among Bible scholars who waited in great suspense for the wood to be analyzed and dated.

Preliminary analyses of Navarra's five-foot beam recovered from the jaws of the 35-foot deep crevasse indicated that the wood was actually from the Ark.

Scientists, wood experts and Bible scholars agreed on several observed surface features establishing the wood's authenticity, says Richard Bliss, University of Wisconsin adjunct science professor. He mentions these surface features of the wood:

> The wood is dark in color like the wood fragments seen by Parrot (1829) and Wells (1933) at the Echmiadzin monastery. The dark description also matches that of the wood recovered by James Bryce in 1876.

> The Navarra wood sample is a structural beam and impregnated with bituminous pitch. It has mortise and tenon joints. And it's definitely hand-hewn and squared. These observable features square with the Biblical account and pre-dynastic ship building methods.[1]

But these surface characteristics do not tell us the age of the wood nor give any other data that would provide further evidence of authenticity.

Biblical historians generally agree that the great Flood occurred about 5,000 years ago. If the wood could be tested for age, and it could be determined that it was in fact 5,000 years old, then Navarra could be sure the wood was from the Ark.

Wood Tested

In 1956 Navarra had several tests conducted on his 1955 wood sample to determine its age and other information. He submitted the wood to four testing procedures, which could be cross-referenced. They were the same testing methods used to date such ancient artifacts as King Tut's coffin, Egyptian canoes and prehistoric wooden tools.

The test methods determined the *degree of lignite or coal formation, gain in wood density, cell modification* and the *degree of fossilization*. From the results, an age calculation could be made.

In our own research we contacted several scientists in different fields to determine how these four tests would have been performed.

We told scientists that we wanted to recreate for a motion picture four testing procedures used to determine the age of a piece of wood believed to be from Noah's Ark.

Scientists Leery

Unfortunately, the mention of "Noah's Ark" were trigger words; they declined to cooperate and usually denied that such tests even existed.

We know that the tests Navarra used in fact did exist because we know that they had been used frequently in archaeology before the invention of Carbon 14. Also, we had the European test results in our hands.

We pursued our investigation to learn the procedures and instruments used, finally locating two geology postgraduate students who were working on their Ph.D.'s, one at the University of California, Los Angeles, and the other at the University of Pennsylvania. Both agreed to give us the information, but did not want their names used. One felt that any publicity might jeopardize his educational goals. We began to feel like we were obtaining top secret information, although the tests are rather uncomplicated and can be conducted in almost any well-equipped laboratory. The key is an expert who knows how to evaluate and interpret the data.

The Tests

Rather than take up pages to run through the various tests, we'll mention the purpose of each test and the equipment used. This will help you better to understand the test results on the Navarra wood samples.

The *degree of lignite formation* is to determine the present stage of conversion of wood to coal. A very thin section of the wood is mounted on a slide and examined by using a petrographic microscope or an X-ray defractometer, a type of electron microscope that measures the angle of reflection of the X-rays off the wood.

Another method to determine *degree of lignite formation* is to treat the wood sample with alcohol or organic solvents to destroy the cell material leaving only the coal or carbon. If it dissolves very little cell material, the sample is highly coalified; and if it dissolves a lot of cell material, it is only slightly coalified.

The *degree of fossilization* is the determination of the amount of water salts contained in a wood sample, thereby telling us what stage of fossilization the sample has reached.

This test is performed by treating the wood samples with acids or alcohols, then examining the specimen under microscope for traces of calcium carbonate or silica. The fuller the cells with these minerals, the greater the degree of fossilization.

The *gain in wood density* is to determine how compact the wood is and whether the wood will float or sink in water. To determine the gain in density, the sample is weighed in the air using a Metler analytical balance, then weighed in a beaker of water. A gain in density, due to compression or contraction, can cause a sample to sink. Also, a piece of wood that has undergone any degree of fossilization will show a gain in wood density.

Cell modification tests determine the degree of cell collapse and cell wall chemical changes. Wood cells may become elongated or may combine with each other. This modification can be charted for age.

A slide of the wood sample is examined under a microscope for cell changes. The key factor in this test is the interpretation of what is seen through the microscope such as what caused the cells to change shape, to combine with other cells or to collapse.

Who Conducted Tests

The Navarra tests were conducted at the National Museum of Natural History in Paris, the National Center of Scientific Research in Paris, the Forestry Institute of Research in Madrid, the Center for Forestry Research and Analysis in Paris, the Department of Anthropology & Prehistoric Studies at the University of Bordeaux, and at the Cairo Museum in Egypt.

What kind of evidence did these impressive scientific centers unearth about Navarra's wood sample? Let's examine their findings.

The following is an excerpt from the report on Navarra's wood issued by Ed Boureau, Under Director of the National Museum of Natural History:

The wood is blackish in color and comes from a thick trunk. The annual rings have a thickness of from 2 to 4 mm, which for a tree indicates active growth. The wood belongs to the *Quercus* oak group, but has a darker cellular content than present oak woods.[2]

F. Nasera, head of the Forestry Section at the Forestry Institute of Research and Experiments in Madrid, Spain, explains that the sample is "a hard and compact wood with a density of 1.100." Nasera goes on to explain how the Institute determined the age of Navarra's sample:

Two traits may serve as the base for age calculation, with all the margin for error proper in this case to ascertain the possible age of the wood examined: the density and the color.

183

The density of the sample seems to have a value of 1.100, and as the normal density of this wood (*Quercus*) is between 0.800 and 0.850, it is evident that this sample is in the lignitization phase (coal formation) of fossilization.

The color, which tells unquestionably the raised percentage of tannin normal in oak wood, confirms on its part its previous state.

Consequently, one can suppose the age of the wood sample given varies around 5,000 years.[3]

Nasera also said in his report that from the piece of wood examined, one cannot ascertain the category of tools—whether iron, copper or stone—used to shape the Navarra sample.

An analysis of the wood in the Department of Anthropology and Prehistoric studies at the University of Bordeaux in France, tells us much more about the prehistoric nature of the wood. G. Malvesin-Fabre, director of the Prehistoric Division, explains their findings:

The block seems to us as very lignitic and, on the other hand, corroded and cracked on the surface. Our impression of a very extensive lignation was confirmed under the Zeiss stereo-microscope. Also the cells are clearly elongated.

According to the annual rings, this wood fragment was taken from a tree whose heartwood attained a diameter of at least 50 cm.

It is a deciduous leaf ... fibrous oak, *Quercus cerris* L. This beautiful tree of the peri-Mediterranean region has moreover a heavy and compact wood, of an average density of 0.925 which, in times of wooden ships, was used in the Orient for naval construction.

It is nevertheless permissible to hesitate between this oak and the *Quercus castaneifolia* Mey., from the south and east Mediterranean regions whose wood shows an extremely close anatomical structure, with an average density of 0.938.

The analysis of the annual rings suggests a tree with an active growth, having grown in a forest of little density with humid springs.

The advanced stage of lignitization deserves to be noted; one can conclude that this wood was subject to conditions very favorable to fossilization during a period dating to a remote antiquity.[4]

From the analyses by Dr. Fabre and Mr. Nasera, we can conclude some other facts about the wood sample, according to Professor Bliss. "The corroded and cracked surface indicates deterioration by freezing and thawing as well as water soaking," he says. "The wood will no longer float on water because of its gain in density. Also it has undergone some lignite formation and fossilization. The elongated cells in the specimen most likely resulted from glacial pressure on the wood.

"A heartwood of 50 centimeters means Navarra's sample came from a tree about five feet in diameter with a height of about 150 feet. Also the particular *Quercus* variety mentioned by Dr. Fabre is a *white oak* and grows only in the Mediterranean region where Noah is believed to have built the Ark."[5]

The Center of Forestry Research and Analysis in Paris also agreed that the sample was oak and gave it an age of about 4,500 years old.

Concerning the tests done at the Cairo Museum, Navarra says, "when we passed through Egypt, I showed the wood to an expert at the Cairo Museum. Though I told him nothing about where the wood came from, he estimated it to be 4,000 to 6,000 years old."[6] No actual scientific testing was done at the Cairo Museum.

Recently in America, the University of California released results of a testing procedure conducted on the Navarra wood by means of measuring the Carbon 14 in the wood. The results were very similar to those obtained by the Geochron Laboratories in Cambridge, Mass., and those that resulted from the Carbon 14 tests conducted at the University of Pennsylvania. All dates obtained varied between 1,250 and 1,700 years—*a rather large fluctuation for tests on the same sample and far short of 5,000 years.*

Carbon 14 Dating Casts Doubts

As a result of the Carbon 14 dating tests, serious doubt was cast on the authenticity of Navarra's wood sample. Many critics immediately claimed the wood could not be from Noah's Ark even though all the other pieces of the puzzle pointed to that fact.

While researching this book, we decided to look into Carbon 14 dating to determine its validity. We wanted to know how the test is conducted. Is the method based on any assumptions? Has it ever been in error?

We had heard that some research scientists criticized Carbon 14 for giving too old an age to many artifacts. But with the Navarra wood sample, the Carbon 14 gave an age that was too young, something not often cited as a criticism. We had a real investigation on our hands.

To understand Carbon 14 testing, we must first understand how it is formed and how it reacts in living things.

The Earth's upper atmosphere is subjected to continuous bombardment by cosmic rays, which give rise to particles called neutrons, which in turn collide with atoms of nitrogen. As a result of the collisions, atoms of radioactive carbon are formed. These are heavier than the ordinary ones whose atomic weight is 12, whereas the new ones are 14.

These radioactive carbon atoms burn to carbon dioxide, which then mixes with the air; the percentage is nearly constant all over the world. It follows that the carbon of all living things tends to contain the same percentage of Carbon 14 in extremely small amounts.

When a living thing dies, it ceases to draw any more carbon from the atmospheric carbon dioxide and its radioactivity dies away steadily. The rate of this "dying away"

186

follows a logarithmic law: half of it is gone in 5745 ± 50 years.[7]

"The small standard deviation of 50 years on the half-life is of no real importance," says British scientist Dr. Frederick A. Filby. "The assumption that the Carbon 14 content of the atmosphere has been constant over a period of 30,000 years is open to much wider question."[8]

A published article by R. E. Lingenfelter, in 1963, has shown that the present rate of formation of Carbon 14 is greater than it used to be, and by quite an important factor, which would make radiocarbon dates too high.

Lingenfelter has shown that over the last ten solar cycles the production rate of Carbon 14 atoms has exceeded the decay rate. This means that there is not a true radioactive equilibrium in the atmosphere. If such a variation had occurred over the whole of the time since the Ice Age, it can be shown by calculation that a specimen 10,000 years old would give a radiocarbon age of 30,000 years.[9]

"Another assumption on which Carbon 14 is based is that specimens have neither gained nor lost radiocarbon by physical or chemical means during the long periods that they have remained buried," says Dr. Filby, a chemist. "In fact, it is known that specimens can lose their heavier isotopes of carbon preferentially to solutions containing Carbon 12."[10]

Let's consider some radiocarbon dates to see just how reliable these datings are. A piece of charred bread from Pompeii, destroyed in A.D. 79, was given an age of 1,850 ± 30 years—a near perfect dating.

Wrappings from the pots of the Dead Sea Scrolls (about 1,890 years old) gave figures of 1,920 to 1,965 years—too high a difference. Columbia University obtained 1,430 ± 150 years for wood from a Sequoia tree when the true age of 1,377 ± 4 had been found by counting rings.

For much older specimens, the results become considerably less reliable. Material from the Grotto de la Garenne, said to be Magdalenian in date, were given ages of 9,000, 11,000, 13,000 and 15,000 years B.P. (Before

Present) when these artifacts should have been contemporary.[11]

"It is obvious that some very old specimens are showing dates that are considerably too high due either to loss of Carbon 14, or to the fact that there was less Carbon 14 in the atmosphere in those days," says Dr. Filby.[12]

We've firmly established that Carbon 14 frequently gives dates too old on artifacts beyond 2,000 years of age and becomes a totally unreliable dating method on artifacts of great antiquity. But we still have not solved the problem of Navarra's wood sample being put at such a young age by Carbon 14.

Carbon 14 Method Itself Doubted

In the 20 years since the introduction of radiocarbon dating by W. F. Libby, some 91 universities and laboratories in 25 different countries have dated over 15,000 independent specimens of once-living matter. Carbon 14 as an accurate dating method virtually went unchallenged until 1954, when Dr. Melvin A. Cook, at that time professor of metallurgy at the University of Utah, proved major discrepancies in the time clock of Carbon 14, resulting sometimes in preposterous test conclusions. His proven discrepancies not only rocked the scientific testing community, but caused Dr. Libby to re-examine his Carbon 14 dating process and to make an unsuccessful attempt to answer Cook's criticism.

Dr. Cook, the 1968 Nitro-Nobel Gold Medal winner for his inventions of slurry explosives, which are today rapidly replacing Alfred Nobel's dynamite, believes the Carbon 14 test results indicating an extremely young age on Navarra's Ark sample to be inaccurate because the assumptions on which Carbon 14 is based are not applicable to this piece of wood.

"*Living* mollusks are sometimes found deficient in Carbon 14 to such an extent as to appear to have been dead as long as 3,000 years," says Dr. Cook. "This is due to carbonate-ion exchange in salt water in contact with old calcite and dolomite deposits. These mollusks are in an environment of old carbonates, and during their life cycle, they assimilate those carbonates that have no radiocarbon in them, rather than to be in steady state with the atmosphere.[13]

"The reverse (dates that are too low) will also happen by involving carbonate-ion exchange in freshwater lakes which become high in alkalinity and thus tend to absorb carbon dioxide from the air to form new calcites and dolomites—which explains the discrepancies in dating of bristlecone pine," says Dr. Cook.

"The bristlecone pine is always dated by tree ring dates older—as much as 2,000 or 3,000 years older—than the date obtained by radiocarbon dating. It's due to the contamination of the bristlecone pine with newer material . . . diffusion of new carbon into the cells of the bristlecone pine.[14]

"We can't really use the Carbon 14 dating method to date the Navarra wood. It can't be used unless we know exactly the conditions that the wood has been under during its existence.

"That's a volcanic mountain, and the wood has been taken from water subjected to the gasses and the solutions from volcanism. It also shows fossilization, which means there has been ion exchange within the wood.

"All it would take for this test to be completely off would be to have excess carbonate-ion exchange, and the carbonate-ion in this case would be from fresh water deposits where the wood was found submerged. Carbon 14 dating would make it appear younger than it really is. And I think this is probably the explanation of the fact that the dating on this wood is only 1,300 to 1,700 years." states Dr. Cook

"Also just contamination of the wood sample alone would make it impossible to really date it by the radiocarbon method," Dr. Cook says. "The sample has undergone a lot of different environments that would promote the possibility of ion exchange."[15]

After researching the Carbon 14 dating process and all the claims and criticisms of the four tests used by Navarra, we tend to bank on the accuracy of Navarra's testing procedures.

Radiocarbon dating leaves too much to be desired—erroneous assumptions, unreliable tests of accuracy—on artifacts of great antiquity, and ion exchanges, that create age dates that are either too low or too high. Carbon 14 just isn't a suitable method for determining the age of Navarra's wood.

Even if we accepted the existing radiocarbon dates on his sample and totally ignored the ion-exchange factors, the range of dates from $1,250 \pm 50$ to $1,700 \pm 50$ years is suspect because a 450 year range exists between three tests on the same sample.

After all, the radiocarbon experts tell us that dates on artifacts under two thousand years of age nearly always date accurately with a possible fluctuation of under 100 years—not 450 years.

Although the four tests performed on Navarra's wood are not used much since the invention of radiocarbon dating, they have been widely used by archaeologists in the past to arrive at reliable age dates as well as to gain substantial amounts of other information about the artifact—as we have seen earlier in this chapter.

From our examination of the evidence, we are in agreement with Navarra that he does, in fact, have a piece of wood from Noah's Ark.

What's your conclusion?

Footnotes
Chapter 12

1. Bliss, Richard, interview, March 1976.
2. Navarra, Fernand, *Noah's Ark: I Touched It*, (Logos International, Plainfield, N.J., 1974), Appendix, p. 124.
3. *Ibid.*, p. 127.
4. *Ibid.*, pp. 128-132.
5. Bliss, *op. cit.*, interview.
6. Navarra, *op. cit.*, p. 68.
7. E. Hughes and W. Mann. *International Journal of Applied Radiation and Isotopes*, (1964), Vol. 15, p. 97.
8. Filby, Frederick A., *The Flood Reconsidered* (Zondervan Publishing Corp., Grand Rapids, MI, 1970), p. 13-14.
9. Lingenfelter, R. E., *Review Geophysics*, (1963), Vol. 1, pp. 35-55.
10. Filby, *op. cit.*, p. 14.
11. *Ibid.*
12. *Ibid.*
13. Statements made during an interview with Dr. Melvin A. Cook in Salt Lake City, Utah, February 1976.
14. *Ibid.*
15. *Ibid.*

CHAPTER 13

Satellite, Spy Plane and CIA Involvement

Virtually every expedition to Mt. Ararat for the past 200 years has been "on foot," meaning that modern expeditions have had to do without such modern equipment as airplanes and helicopters.

Because Ararat is in a restricted military zone on the Turkish-Soviet border, the Turks have consistently refused to grant permits allowing the use of aircraft in the fear planes might accidentally drift across the Soviet border and create an international incident or be shot down by the Russians.

So the methods of exploring Mt. Ararat haven't changed much since Friedrich Parrot's first climb up the mountain in 1829. In addition, the same hassles have persisted: unreliable guides, frequent harassment by government officials, inclement weather and other problems.

With the birth of the aerospace industry, a new exploration method for Noah's Ark developed. We now have spy planes, mapping satellites and highly sophisticated military satellites, all of which are probably capable of detecting or photographing the Ark on Mt. Ararat.

Has the aerospace industry and Cold-War spying technology detected the Ark on Mt. Ararat? And why is the government interested in Noah's Ark? Even more intriguing, why are the CIA and its Russian spy counterpart, KGB, interested in Ararat expeditions?

Satellite Finds Shape

Satellite photography did not come to the attention of Ark-eologists until about mid-1973 when Thomas B. Turner, a manager at the McDonnell Douglas Astronautics Company, St. Louis, contacted Dr. John Montgomery to tell him about a satellite photo that possibly showed the Ark.

It seems that an employee of the Earth Resources Observation Satellite Center in Sioux Falls, South Dakota, found a peculiar rectangular shape, apparently foreign to the mountain, while checking the imagery transmitted by an Earth Resources Technology Satellite (ERTS).

"Most remarkable was the location of the rectangle: in the very quadrant of the mountain where previous ground sightings (of the Ark) had been concentrated," says Dr. Montgomery. "The government employee had not known this when he located the strange shape."[1]

Describing the shape, Dr. Montgomery says, "Rectangles or straight lines are not produced naturally. When remote satellite sensing techniques are used to determine whether one is dealing with artifacts or with natural land formations, the supposition is that when straight lines are seen of the type observed in this photo, it's a human product.[2]

"As a result of this information, Senator Frank E. Moss, who is chairman of the Senate Aeronautical and Space Sciences Committee, made a public announcement that satellite confirmation of the existence of the Ark might very well have been provided," says Dr. Montgomery.[3]

To understand satellite photography better, we need to know some background information about the satellite which took the intriguing photo.

ERTS-1 was launched into an orbit 450 miles above Earth on July 23, 1972. Included among its functional systems was a multi-spectral scanner (MSS) which continually scans an area of the Earth's surface one hundred nautical miles wide along the satellite's orbit. The imagery yielded covers in each instance 10,000 nautical square miles.

The satellite's transmitted data is originally processed at the Goddard Space Flight Center, Maryland. The wave length bands are reconstituted by photographic or optical means, or by using computer analysis to classify the data in a digital magnetic tape format.

But did the ERTS photograph really show Noah's Ark? We decided to investigate this assumption more thoroughly. It would be a significant step forward in the search for Noah's Ark. We made a startling discovery.

Who Saw What?

First, it was apparently Dr. Montgomery who concluded the "foreign object" was probably Noah's Ark and set up Senator Moss to make the public announcement.

Senator Moss' announcement, made before a meeting of the American Congress on Surveying and Mapping in Salt Lake City in Februrary, 1974, was based "on a confidential memorandum he received from Dr. John Montgomery, a professor at Trinity Divinity School . . ." and not based on any NASA analysis.[4]

Furthermore, we learned that "the government employee" at the Earth Resources Observation Satellite Center in Sioux Falls, South Dakota, was not a qualified ERTS photo analyst but a mail room and supply clerk.[5]

Les Gaver, a NASA official in Washington, D.C., told the *Los Angeles Times* (May 26, 1974) that it was 'fairly unlikely' that an object the size of the Ark could be detected in a photo taken from that altitude.

"Our people feel that they don't see that (an ark), or that they don't interpret the photo that way," he said.

Whether the satellite was even capable of spotting something as small as the Ark was investigated by us. We contacted aerospace scientists familiar with the ERTS capabilities.

This is what one NASA System Engineer concluded:

A problem is that by examining an ERTS photo, one can deduce the specification of the camera that took it. This has been a particular problem for us at NASA. As a result we have had to use less than the best cameras and film on multimillion dollar space missions.

The various pieces of equipment that the sensor data has to go through in the photo processes all contribute some degradation to the resolution quality of the MSS data.

A human observer hypothetically placed at the MSS output which is in the satellite could recognize adjacent fields of wheat and mildewed barley, if they each exceeded 100 meters in width. If he were viewing a reproduced photo image from the MSS data, he could recognize the same fields if they exceeded 300 meters in width.

The ability of the Ark to be detected by the MSS would be based on several factors: contrast of the Ark material against the background, size of the Ark or exposed portions, and position of the Ark with respect to the direction of the satellite sensor scans.

The Ark dimension is approximately 135 × 25 meters from the top view. These are at the very limits of the 50-90 meter ground resolution of ERTS. Under optimal conditions with the Ark fully exposed it could appear as a single dark dot in the image.

If the Ark has been broken and the material distributed over a large area of the ice field, a larger signal could be detected depending on the density and depth of the materials in the ice.

Since very high resolution data acquired by the U.S. Air Force reconnaissance satellites is classified and currently unavailable to the public, it is unlikely that greater resolution imagery will be available until the launch of the next generation of Earth Resources Technology Satellites ... later in this decade.[6]

Special Photo Analysis

Dr. Montgomery had the photo subjected to special analysis at the Center for Remote Sensing at the Environmental Research Institute of Michigan. After various types of enlargements they were unable to draw any definitive conclusions:

The anomalous rectangular pattern is apparently caused by sunlight striking the terrain in an area otherwise shadowed by the ridge or glacial ice to the east. This can be considered due to a rectangular object or ridge projecting upward out of the shadowed area or as due to a notch or break in the ridge of ice to the east causing this peculiar shadow on the otherwise smooth terrain.[7]

It also appears now that Dr. Montgomery recognizes that the rectangle in the photograph is too large to be the *intact* Ark when he says in the latest pocket edition of his book, "The overall rectangle is larger than the dimensions of the Biblical Ark. There is a smaller, perceptibly whiter area within the total rectangle, but the resolution capabilities of the imagery do not permit determining its size. The ERTS data is by no means definitive."[8]

The ERTS photo containing the unique little rectangle, designated the intact Ark by Dr. Montgomery via Senator Moss' public announcement, reveals no such proof.

Other Photos Analyzes

Dr. Montgomery did have some later ERTS photos of the mountain subjected to remote sensing analysis at the Geophysical Institute of the University of Alaska in Fairbanks.

Dr. John M. Miller's report (September 3, 1974) on these ERTS photos intrigues us because the area photographed is close to where Navarra found his timbers in 1955 and 1969:

There is another spot that could be of greater significance as a potential anomalous area. It is the somewhat circular, light-blue region in the northwest quadrant of the snow field. Such a light blue-gray color tone compared with more pure white surroundings frequently is indicative of melting or less thick ice and snow.

This is an effect that imbedded, dark-colored wood might have in the summer upon the ice that surrounds it. While the discolored area is much too large for the

Ark itself, there is the possibility that it no longer is intact. If the wood is broken, deteriorated, and scattered a bit, it might have an effect over an area much larger than its original dimensions.[9]

Navarra has always contended that the Ark will no longer be found totally intact. Although its hull may be intact at a higher elevation, he believes much of the ancient structure is scattered in and about the ice pack in which he found his samples.

Realizing that the ERTS spacecraft was not capable of photographing a visually identifiable Ark and that Dr. Montgomery's analysis of the photos by two independent laboratories produced inconclusive evidence, we decided to contact the Earth Resources Observation Satellite Center in South Dakota to determine if it could perform any type of electronic computer analysis of the satellite data gathered over Mt. Ararat.

Principal Systems Analyst Dr. Frederick Waltz, performed for us a computer analysis of the reflective light patterns observed by the ERTS spacecraft as movie cameras filmed the scene for our motion picture, "In Search of Noah's Ark."

As satellite signal data was fed into the computer, a total visual image of what the cameras recorded flashed onto a television screen. The pushing of a few computer programming buttons transformed the image to a close-up of Mt. Ararat and the surrounding area.

Next the programmer put an electronic rectangle over the side of the mountain where the Ark is supposed to be located. They enlarged this area 25 times and this enlarged rectangle appeared in the upper right corner of the screen. Within this rectangle were many smaller rectangular blocks known as picture elements, each representing one acre of territory.

Then with the assistance of an electronic pointer which was reduced to the size of a single picture element and inserted into one of the picture element blocks, the computer operator was able to study the reflective light pattern of each individual picture element.

The programmer asked the computer to indicate all areas on or near Mt. Ararat that had the same reflective pattern as that indicated in each individual picture element. Each time a picture element was tested, dozens of green lights appeared over the entire Ararat area.

Finally the pointer was moved to the specific picture element where the Ark is believed to be located. When the computer was activated, it was the only spot on the mountain to turn green—indicating that it was the only area on the mountain with that specific reflective pattern.

At that point, our film's narrator Brad Crandall put the question to Dr. Waltz—could this be Noah's Ark?

"I certainly could not discount that possibility," replied Dr. Waltz.

Although the ERTS spacecraft orbiting 450 miles above Earth is not capable of visually photographing something as small as an intact Ark hull on Mt. Ararat, military spy satellites do have that capability.

Satellites Could Show Ark

Satellites used to verify whether the Russians are keeping their part of the SALT arms limitation agreement are equipped with television cameras, infrared, and other sophisticated sensors that can operate day or night, in any weather. From roughly 600 miles up, they can monitor movements with great clarity; or if activities are undercover, can watch related patterns of movement, according to statements made during a February, 1976, (Washington, D.C.) news conference with Malcolm R. Currie, director of the Pentagon's Defense Research and Engineering Division.

We have been told by reliable Pentagon sources that these highly sophisticated military spy satellites are capable of photographing the Ark not as a mere dot but as a well-defined structure.

Our Defense Department source says that military photos of the Ark probably exist in Pentagon files, to which civilians would never have access.

About reliance on satellite photos for detecting the

Ark, Dr. Miller observes, "Satellite remote sensing of the environment must be coupled with data acquired from aircraft as well as with surface observations in order to be completely effective."[10]

Has any aircraft observed the Ark in recent times? Since normal aircraft are not permitted to fly in the vicinity of Mt. Ararat, the question would apply to American spy plane observations.

It had long been rumored that U-2 spy plane pilot Francis Gary Powers, while flying secret photographic missions over the Soviet Union, spotted the Ark on Mt. Ararat. But in an interview with Powers, he indicated he did not see the Ark while in the air or in photos, although he admits he seldom saw very many of the photos.

Spy Plane Photos

But one Ark researcher, John Morris, has done a considerable amount of research into spy plane photos and Noah's Ark.

"During the 1950's and 60's spy plane pilots saw and photographed the Ark on Mt. Ararat," says Morris. "I've personally interviewed the pilot of one of these planes and an analyst who viewed several spy plane photos, which he said showed the Ark."[11]

Morris has contacted Defense Department officials, with the help of Congressional representatives, in an attempt to acquire copies of these photos. So far his attempts have failed.

"Even though the pictures would be 10 to 15 years old, the military is not inclined to release them, probably because Ararat is in a restricted military zone and any mission that would take pictures of this area would be a classified mission," says Morris.[12]

"Releasing photos is difficult for several reasons," states a high NASA official. "One is the system of classification. For example, the photo wanted may not contain classified information, but was no doubt taken by an aircraft or satellite on a photographic mission that was classified. If one starts to declassify photos here and there, in effect, the system of classification crumbles."

We have learned that one apparent reason for the reluctance to release photos is that some of them may show the Russian missile fuel depot and launching pad which is located less than forty miles from Ararat and said to be visible from Mt. Ararat.

The Spy Connection

Naturally, when you hear about military or other kinds of international spying, you automatically think of the CIA or the Russian KGB, and in this case, a connection exists between the interests of these organizations and expeditions to Mt. Ararat in search of Noah's Ark.

The first mention of CIA involvement was in 1970 when the SEARCH Foundation expedition to Mt. Ararat was scuttled because the Turkish government revoked its climbing permits.

Other reasons also influenced the cancellation of SEARCH's permits, but the major factor was Russian pressure on Turkish officials.

Articles in *Pravda*, the Russian government's official newspaper, accused the expedition of "coming to spy and not to dig." The Soviets charged that American explorers left tools on Mt. Ararat intended to collect information about nuclear tests inside Russia.[13]

The accusation shook public and government opinion in Turkey. Articles even in many Turkish newspapers claimed the U. S. Central Intelligence Agency was involved in the project.[14]

One American newspaper account expanded on the story:

Former Turkish intelligence chief, Adm. Sezai Okrunt, can hardly believe that the expedition is serious.

The idea that anyone would still take the Bible as literal truth is too much for non-Bible readers to understand.

Perhaps the expedition is a Central Intelligence Agency (CIA) plot, Okrunt indicated.

Turkish officials commented that allowing such expeditions runs the risk of provoking the Russians.[15]

CIA Involvement

In our research we did in fact discover that the CIA was involved in some of the expeditions during the 1960's. We acquired our information from a recently active Ararat explorer who said he was approached in the 1970's to work for the CIA while on Ararat expeditions. Our informant says he declined the offer. He has asked us to keep his name confidential because he hopes to make future explorations of Mt. Ararat.

"While sitting in an office in the CIA headquarters near Washington, D.C., I was informed that some of the explorers during the 1960's were CIA informants or employes," says our source. "However, the CIA people did not tell me what function they performed for the agency.

"In the same meeting, I was asked to work for them while on one of my upcoming expeditions. I refused to cooperate or get involved.

"Their request came as such a sudden shock, that my first reaction was to say no before even hearing them out as to what they wanted me to do. You hear about people being CIA informants, but when you're asked to be one, pointblank, it's frightening and I instinctively said no."

Aerospace technology has increased the dimension of the search for Noah's Ark. At the same time, it has created a tremendous amount of international intrigue.

In the final analysis, space technology has brought to a level of scientific confirmation, the existence of Noah's Ark.

Footnotes
Chapter 13

1. Montgomery, John Warwick, *The Quest for Noah's Ark* (Dimension Books, Minneapolis, MN, 1974), p. 316.

2. Statements made during an interview with Dr. John Warwick Montgomery, March 1976.

3. Montgomery interview, *op. cit.*

4. United Press International, "Noah's Ark Seen?" *The Register,* Santa Ana, CA, Feb. 22, 1974.

5. Interview with NASA officials, Sioux Falls, South Dakota.

6. Waltz, Edward L., "Space Age Archaeology", *Bible and Spade,* Autumn, 1974. Waltz is a systems engineer in the Aerospace System Division of Bendix Corp.

7. Montgomery, *op. cit.,* p. 354.

8. *Ibid.,* p. 317.

9. *Ibid.,* p. 320.

10. Miller, John M. and Belon, Albert E., *Remote Sensing by Satellite* (Geophysical Institute of the University of Alaska, Fairbanks, 1973), p. 12.

11. Statements made during an interview with John Morris, February, 1976.

12. *Ibid.*

13. Fessler, Gordon, "Russ Ban Mt. Ararat to Noah's U.S. Spies," *Anaheim Bulletin,* (Anaheim, CA, August 29, 1970), p. 1. The article was filed by the *Bulletin's* Washington Bureau.

14. Associated Press, "Turks Bar Expedition to Find Noah's Ark," *The Register,* (Santa Ana, CA, July 13, 1970), p. 1.

15. Fessler, *op. cit.,* p. 1.

CHAPTER 14

The Mystery of Noah's Ark Resolved

At the beginning of this book, we explained that there were many undisputed facts relating to an ancient mystery on Mt. Ararat in Eastern Turkey. Throughout the book, we have presented evidence that connects these undisputed facts to the Biblical Great Deluge and a man named Noah, who survived with his cargo of ainmals aboard an Ark.

But more than correlating the undisputed facts of this case with the Bible, we've presented evidence in many relevant areas to substantiate the connection. We have dealt with the historical accuracy of the Bible, the anthropological evidence for a great deluge, the scientific evidence supporting a universal flood and environmental conditions needed to produce a flood.

We have told of documented carly sightings of Noah's Ark, the treachery of Mt. Ararat, expeditions and sightings of the 1800's, eyewitness accounts that furnished detailed descriptions of the Ark, 20th century expeditions and sightings, the Navarra wood finds, and the use of spy planes and satellites to confirm the existence of Noah's Ark on Mt. Ararat.

Finally, we have analyzed the Ark's construction, showed how the survivors lived aboard the vessel and after they disembarked; scrutinized the analysis of the Navarra wood and documented the international intrigue surrounding the Ark.

Sighting Statistics

Our research indicates that 200 people in 23 separate sightings since 1856 have seen Noah's Ark on Mt.

Ararat.[1] We have the Biblical and historical accounts, the archaeological records, the anthropological accounts, the scientific evidence, local accounts from villagers, eyewitness accounts, the spectacular discovery of wood by Navarra, and the spy plane-satellite confirmations to verify the existence of Noah's Ark.

The evidence for the Flood and for the existence of the Ark is overwhelming.

We live in a world where many ideas are accepted on far less evidence than we have accumulated. We felt it necessary to present all the available evidence in order for you to arrive at a fair and decisive verdict. No sacred cows have mooed in our investigation. We feel that we have shattered groundless theories, widely held false opinions and poorly researched conclusions.

More than just presenting accounts of sightings and tales of expeditions, we have described how the scientific community has carefully examined every aspect of the Ark account and the evidence relating to it and has had to admit that this, the greatest story in the Bible, is true!

Our conclusion is that the Ark is on Mt. Ararat. Why isn't anyone sending teams to the mountain, attempting major excavations? Don't we have the technological know-how to recover wood from beneath 30 to 100 feet of ice? We not only have the know-how, but an operational plan and the specialized equipment to do the excavation. *But we must wait.*

Turks Clamp Down

In April, 1974, the Turkish government officially announced a ban on travel by foreigners to Mt. Ararat, according to an article in *Christianity Today* (May 24, 1974) which states:

All new maps printed by travel agencies are required to indicate Mt. Ararat as an off-limits area to foreigners. No detailed explanation was given by authorities; the Turkish interior ministry merely cited problems caused by increasing numbers wanting to climb the mountain "under varying pretenses." It did not say what the pretenses were. . . .

Since the 1970 well-publicized SEARCH Foundation's climbing permit cancellation, most expeditions have had great difficulty in obtaining permits. Very few expeditions have got on the mountain.

Turkish Reasons

Let's examine some of the reasons Turkish officials give for revoking expedition climbing permits over the past five years.

Associated Press and Turkish government news dispatches from Ankara, dated July 13, 1970, disclosed the following reasons for the cancellation of the SEARCH climbing permits:[2]

1. The Turkish government's unstable political situation and fear of international criticism.

2. Soviet newspapers and some Turkish newspapers claim that the U.S. Central Intelligence Agency was involved in the expedition.

3. The government's fear of possible foreign involvement in resurgent separatism among Kurds, who live in the vicinity of Mt. Ararat.

4. Nervousness in Moslem Turkey about the connection of the Christian church with the SEARCH Foundation.

5. A Turkish crackdown on smuggling ancient treasures out of the country and into American and European museums.

6. SEARCH's lack of cooperation with other groups seeking to do further research on the same project.

7. A diplomatic incident involving one of the SEARCH team members.

Mount Ararat is located in what is referred to as a restricted military zone, probably because of its close proximity to the Turkish-Russian border and because the Russians have a military missile facility about 40 miles from the mountain. It has long been known by the Russians that most of the American reconnaissance of the Soviet Union originates at U.S. occupied bases in Turkey. The recent agreement permitting Americans to re-occupy 22 bases in Turkey was only reached after the United States agreed to share all acquired reconnaissance information with the Turkish government. Naturally the Russians automatically suspect that any American expedition on or near Mt. Ararat would be for spying purposes.

From 1970 to 1974, when Interior Minister Oguz Asiltürk announced the ban on all expeditions, American groups headed by Eryl Cummings, John Montgomery and John Morris and representatives of the Texas Holy Ground Center were able to get permission to climb the mountain.

Ugly American

Bart LaRue, president of Janus Pictures of Hollywood, made an illegal expedition up Mt. Ararat in 1974. To that infamous event, many attribute stricter controls against granting permits.

"LaRue adopted the ways of a smuggler, a con man and a crook to do it, and he's subject to arrest if he ever returns to Turkey," commented one national newspaper which published his story.[3]

"We laid out nearly $2,000 in bribes. One of the biggest bribes I laid out was to a military post near Mt. Ararat. They took $500 to look the other way as we passed their check point," says LaRue. "I think I will be the last man on the mountain. There won't be another illegal expedition."[4]

We disagree with LaRue that he will be the last man on the mountain, but we are quite sure LaRue won't be back there. It is unfortunate that some people break the rules and ruin possibilities for serious explorers.

206

Internal Reasons

Besides the reasons for canceling the SEARCH expedition and the LaRue episode, other internal reasons are believed to influence the hard line position against expeditions in the immediate future. These include:[5]

> 1. The Moslem religious community might be embarrassed to find the Ark on Mt. Ararat, when Moslem tradition puts the landing of the Ark on another mountain in Turkey.
>
> 2. Russian pressure on Turkey to keep Westerners off Ararat, thus preventing visual spying or the use of electronic gear to spy on the missile depot across the border.
>
> 3. The Kurdish civil war has ended in Iraq and Syria, and civil war renegades are moving to the Ararat area where there is virtually no law and order, creating a danger to foreigners climbing on the mountain.
>
> 4. Opium growers in Eastern Turkey use the road at the base of Mt. Ararat as a major drug smuggling route. In a halfhearted effort at the control of smuggling, the Turks want to keep foreigners out of the area.
>
> 5. Turkish concern over ethnic problems, particularly foreigners siding with the Armenian anti-Turkish attitudes which creates an uneasy situation for the Turkish government.

Any way you look at it, excuses are not in short supply.

One Good Plan

If expeditions could get on the mountain again in the near future, one man has a plan for recovering the Ark. While most explorers still debate whether the Ark is intact or in fragments, still want to investigate sites which usually amount merely to rock formations, Louis "Watcha" McCollum of Danville, Illinois, has a sensible excavation plan.[6]

Not only has McCollum continually refined his plan for the past ten years, he has the necessary aviation equipment to carry it out. He owns McCollum Aviation, which buys, sells, leases and charters aircraft throughout North America. He is believed to be the largest private aircraft owner in the world, with more than 50 planes in his fleet, most of them a variety of passenger jets, supercharged helicopters and a few oddities. In his fleet's jet division are Lears, Citations, Commanders and DH-25's. His helicopter division includes Bell 206's, Hiller FH1100's, and Hughes 500's. His oddity collection of lease planes includes a B-26 wartime attack bomber, a PBY sea-land plane, converted into a flying apartment sleeping 14 people, and a T-33 two-seat fighter plane.

McCollum is not just a big-time airplane salesman. He is a very serious pilot who flew a PBY in the movie "Catch-22," rescued Evel Knievel from the Snake River Canyon, and has flown charter jets for many well-known personalities including Bob Hope, Barry Goldwater, Ted Kennedy, Gene Hackman, Joe Louis, Bobby Riggs, Evel Knievel and three political figures before they became President: Truman, Johnson and Nixon.

About 1965 McCollum became interested in the Ark search and recovery efforts using advanced aviation equipment. He worked up a plan using one of his $75,-000 Bell G3B1 turbo-supercharged helicopters to fly men and equipment to the Ark site. Then in 1969, he became connected with SEARCH Foundation and offered his plan and assistance to the Foundation in their 1970 expedition.

Part of McCollum's plan was to transport his Bell helicopter (the only model at the time capable of operating with crew and load at the 17,000 foot level) to Turkey on his own DC-7 cargo plane, use it on Mt. Ararat, then give it to the Turkish government.

When SEARCH Foundation began to be bogged down with its 1970 expedition, McCollum used his political friendship to arrange a meeting with then President Nixon.

"I had dinner at the White House with the President," says McCollum. "He was quite interested in our Ark expedition plans. I gave him a historical run-down on all the sightings and previous expeditions.

"When he asked what he could do, I told him 'I want permission from the Turkish government for the team to climb Ararat and for me to use my helicopter up there. I want the State Department to pressure the Turks enough to give me permission to operate on Ararat'," says McCollum.

"President Nixon assigned Egil Krogh (later convicted as a Watergate conspirator) to help me get the needed permission. I later learned the President requested from Krogh a full report in writing of all the things I told him concerning the Ark.

"To make a long story short, Krogh pulled some strings at the State Departent, where the man in charge of Turkish Affairs told me they could get me the permit. But with the Cold War state of affairs between the U.S. and Russia, and the anti-Turkish attitude toward the U.S., they practically guaranteed that I would come back in a box," recalls McCollum. "And they said they couldn't offer me any protection."

McCollum says internal problems started cropping up with SEARCH about that time, so he dropped his involvement with the group.

But is McCollum still ready to go if the opportunity becomes available? The answer is yes!

He has sold his Bell G3B1 helicopter, but has replaced it with a Bell 47G3B-1, which he says has more horsepower.

"I keep this new Bell helicopter in my Danville hangar just waiting for the moment when the Turkish government will allow me to use, it," says McCollum, who values the helicopter at $60,000. "I could fly an Ararat mission without any difficulty, for I've spent hours studying the air currents, estimated snowfalls, the mountain ridges and other logistics."

If McCollum gets on Mt. Ararat with his helicopter and supplies, does he have a plan to identify or excavate the Ark?

"I've spent ten years thinking my plan out and have eliminated so many ways it can't be done that there's no need to talk about them," says McCollum.

He has a four point plan for quickly identifying the Ark in the Mt. Ararat ice pack prior to any recovery efforts.

Here's his plan:

1. Use the Bell 47G3B-1 supercharged helicopter to transport men, diamond core power drills (capable of drilling 150 feet) and supplies to the ice pack Ark site. He estimates 10 to 20 tons of supplies and equipment would have to be transported to the site in half-ton loads aboard his helicopter. Then set up camp on the ice pack near the base of operations.

2. Do core drillings on a hit and miss basis to determine the outline of the Ark. Once this is done conduct some drillings in the center with the intent of recovering some bones, hair, grain, pitch or other things left behind when Noah and the animals departed.

3. Next, use a "burning bar" (torch-like device for rapidly demolishing steel, concrete or ice) to dig a tunnel down to the Ark at selected core locations. The burning bar explodes the compacted ice, breaking it into small blocks.

4. Construct geodesic domes over those sites where larger pits are to be dug. The domes will protect the tunnels from filling up with snow and permit the men to work freely, away from harsh outside environmental conditions. Under the domes, all the archaeological excavating and study would be done.

Ark Could Aid Tourism

McCollum believes that when someone is able to excavate the Ark, the Turkish government will probably develop it into a tourist attraction similar to some of the Holy places in Israel. If tourists and Christians throughout the world came to visit the site, it would make a very profitable tourism industry for Turkey.

Some Opinions

But what would the impact and significance of the rediscovery and recovery of Noah's Ark mean to the religious world, the scientific community and possibly the man on the street?

"I think it would have a monumental effect, more upon the scientists than the ordinary people," says Tucson, Arizona, geologist Dr. Clifford Burdick.

"This would prove the basics of Christianity, and we would have to follow the basic moral principles that are in it as to right and wrong," says Fernand Navarra.

"Some of the findings of Biblical archaeology have revolutionized thinking towards the Bible and therefore towards God and towards the faith of man," says Australian archaeologist Dr. Clifford Wilson. "And undoubtedly, if Noah's Ark is again found, I personally believe that it will be a very significant thing, and to many people it will be one of the most significant, startling events of all history."

Theologian Dr. John Montgomery says, "If the Ark is recovered, it will show that even the earliest chapters of

211

Genesis in the Bible are not poetry or myth, but actual history."

"Nothing in archaeology is surprising," says Dr. Phillip Hammond, archaeologist at the University of Utah. "The Dead Sea Scrolls were found when all of us said nothing could be found earlier than the fourth century. So we do get surprised every once in a while. Then you have to sit down and try to figure out the meaning of the surprise."

Dr. Melville B. Grosvenor, the late editor of the *National Geographic* magazine, summed it up: "If the Ark of Noah is ever discovered, it would be the greatest archaeological find in human history, the greatest event since the resurrection of Christ, and it would alter all the currents of scientific thought."

It is sad that the politics of nations stands in the way of man's legacy. It appears that the Ark will remain buried beneath a blanket of ice and snow until the world is at peace or until it's God's time to let it be uncovered.

But we believe that day will come because there is more to this than just the story of a great wooden ship.

It is the story of Noah, a man of strength and foresight, a man with the ability to build a great Ark and survive the Deluge; a man of faith, perhaps more than any of us, who could ignore the ridicule of others and finish a long and difficult task—a man to be respected for his beliefs.

Noah was not only a man of determination before the Flood but surely after it as well when we consider he was faced with the difficult task of reconstructing a civilization from his own family on a totally changed Earth. Like the Lord's direct command to build the Ark, Noah had a command from God to "multiply and replenish the earth." Noah became a farmer near Ararat while his sons and their descendants became metal workers, farmers, nomadic hunters, maritime merchants and empire builders.

Following God's repopulation command to Noah and a brief description of his farming endeavors, the Bible is silent on the specific role played by Noah in the rebuilding of ancient civilizations. The Biblical record deals primarily with the life and times of his descendants. But since Noah lived 350 years or ten generations after the

Great Deluge, he no doubt witnessed many events and is remembered as one of the greatest men in history.

There is a special lesson for each of us in the story of Noah and the Ark. All we have to do is find it for ourselves and apply it!

Footnotes
Chapter 14

1. Lang, Walter, *The Witness of Mount Ararat* (Bible-Science Association, Caldwell, ID, 1974), p. 2.
2. Some information acquired from *The Register*, "Turks Bar Expedition to Find Noah's Ark," (Santa Ana, CA, July 13, 1970).
3. Reining, Paul, "Filming The Ark of Noah Was True Uphill Struggle," *The National Tattler*, Chicago, IL, Feb. 2, 1975, p. 17.
4. *Ibid*.
5. Information compiled during an interview with Ark researcher and Ararat climber John Morris.
6. McCollum information gathered during a March 1976 interview.

EPILOGUE

The geographical distribution of Noah's descendants is given in a brief summary (Gen. 10:1-32). Japheth and his sons settled in the vicinity of the Black and Caspian seas extending westward to Spain (Gen. 10:2-5). The Greek, Indo-Germanic people and other related groups descended from Japheth.

Three sons of Ham went down into Africa (Gen. 10:6-14). Then they spread northward to the land of Shinar and Assyria, building such cities as Nineveh, Calah, Babel, Akkad, and others. Canaan, the fourth son of Ham, settled along the Mediterranean, extending from Sidon down to Gaza and eastward.

Shem and his descendants occupied the area north of the Persian Gulf (Gen. 10:21-31). Elam, Ashur, Aram, and other settlements were associated with the Semites. After 2000 B.C. such cities as Mari and Nahor became leading centers of Semitic culture.

To conclude the early beginnings of man following the Flood, major developments center around the descendants of Shem (Gen. 11:10-32). By following a genealogical framework through ten generations, the Biblical record finally focuses upon Terah. The climax of the Terah generation is the birth of Abram, later known as Abraham (Gen. 17:5), who embodies the beginning of a chosen nation—*the nation of Israel* which occupies the center of interest throughout the rest of the Old Testament.

APPENDIX

Recommended Additional Reading

Noah's Ark: I Touched It by Fernand Navarra
  Logos International, Plainfield, N. J. 07060
Noah's Ark: Fact or Fable? by Violet M. Cummings
  Creation-Science Research Center, San Diego, CA
Noah's Ark: The Search Goes On by John Morris
  Thomas Nelson Inc., Nashville, TN
Adventure on Ararat by John Morris
  Institute for Creation Research, San Diego, CA
The Flood Reconsidered by Frederick A. Filby
  Zondervan Publishing House, Grand Rapids, MI
The Genesis Flood by John Whitcomb, Jr. & Henry Morris
  Presbyterian and Reformed Publishing Co., Philadelphia,
The Quest for Noah's Ark by John Warwick Montgomery
  Bethany Fellowship Inc., Minneapolis, MN
Manners and Customs of the Bible by James M. Freeman
  Logos International, Plainfield, N.J.
Scientific Creationism by Henry M. Morris
  Creation-Life Publishers, San Diego, CA
In the Beginning God by Clifford Wilson
  Baker Book House, Grand Rapids, MI
Speak to the Earth edited by George F. Howe
  Presbyterian and Reformed Publishing Co., Nutley, N.J.
Unger's Bible Handbook by Merrill F. Unger
  Moody Press, Chicago, IL
Light from the Ancient Past by Jack Finegan
  Princeton University Press, Princeton, N.J .
A Symposium on Creation II by Donald W. Patten
  Baker Book House, Grand Rapids, MI
Canyon of Canyons by Clifford Burdick
  Bible-Science Association Inc, Caldwell, ID
Oxford Bible Atlas edited by Herbert G. May
  Oxford University Press, New York, N.Y.

Man's Origin, Man's Destiny by A. E. Wilder Smith
  Harold Shaw Publishers, Wheaton, IL
The Biblical Flood and the Ice Epoch by Donald W. Patten
  Pacific Meridian Publishing Co., Seattle, WA
All the Animals of the Bible Lands by G. S. Cansdale
  Zondervan Publishing House, Grand Rapids, MI
The God of Creation by Theodore H. Epp
  Back to the Bible Broadcast, Lincoln, NE
That Incredible Book . . . The Bible by Clifford Wilson
  Moody Press, Chicago, IL
A Symposium on Creation IV by Donald W. Patten
  Baker Book House, Grand Rapids, MI
Origin & Destiny of the Earth's Magnetic Field by T. Barnes
  Institute for Creation Research, San Diego, CA
Prehistory and Earth Models by Melvin A. Cook
  Max Parrish Co., London, England
Earth's Most Challenging Mysteries by Reginald Daly
  Craig Press, Nutley, N.J.
Evolution: The Fossils Say No! by Duane Gish
  Creation-Life Publishers, San Diego, CA
Genes, Genesis and Evolution by John W. Klotz
  Concordia Publishing House, St. Louis, MO
The Deluge Story in Stone by Byron C. Nelson
  Bethany Fellowship Inc, Minneapolis, MN
The World That Perished by John C. Whitcomb
  Baker Book House, Grand Rapids, MI
The Flood and the Fossils by George Mulfinger, Jr.
  Bob Jones University Press Inc., Greenville, S.C.
Biblical Cosmology and Modern Science by Henry M. Morris
  Presbyterian and Reformed Publishing Co., Nutley, N.J.
Acts and Facts (periodical published monthly)
  Institute for Creation Research, San Diego, CA
Creation Research Quarterly (periodical)
  Creation Research Society, Ann Arbor, MI
Bible and Spade (periodical published quarterly)
  Ballston Spa, N.Y.
Bible-Science Newsletter (periodical published monthly)
  Caldwell, ID

ABOUT THE AUTHORS

Dave Balsiger has authored or ghost authored seven other books including *Noah's Ark: I Touched It, The Satan Seller, It's Good To Know, Beyond Defeat, On The Other Side, One More Time,* and *The Back Side of Satan.* Prior to his writing interests centering on books, he was a feature writer and photographer for the *Anaheim Bulletin* and is currently vice-president of an Anaheim based advertising agency. Due to his literary achievements, he is listed in the 38th edition of *Who's Who in America,* the 3rd edition of *Who's Who in the World,* the 8th edition of *International Authors' and Writers' Who's Who, Gale's Contemporary Authors,* and in *Outstanding Young Men of America for 1976.* On the film, "In Search of Noah's Ark," Balsiger is the historian and technical advisor.

Charles E. Sellier, Jr., was the producer and co-screenplay writer of the motion picture "In Search of Noah's Ark." As a writer-producer, Sellier has been able to achieve his life goal of producing entertainment for the entire family. He has made many highly successful family pictures including "The Life and Times of Grizzly Adams," "The Adventures of Frontier Fremont," "Birth of a Legend," "The Brothers O'Toole," and "The Mysterious Monster." Sellier is currently finishing a new picture about the life of Johnny Appleseed.

Any comments, inquiries for speaking engagements or offers of additional Ark research information or photos should be directed to:

> Dave Balsiger
> Balsiger Literary Service
> P.O. Box 4502
> Anaheim, CA 92801